DIVA 2.0

12 LIFE LESSONS FROM ME FOR YOU!

SHERYL LEE RALPH

wordeee
where words connect

DIVA 2.0

12 LIFE LESSONS FROM ME FOR YOU!

DIVA 2.0: 12 Life Lessons From Me For You!

ISBN: 978-1-959811-02-2 (Paperback)
ISBN: 978-1-959811-03-9 (eBook)
Library of Congress Control Number: 2022920771

Cover Design: Okomota
Interior Design: Amit Dey
Photo Credit Front Cover: Sean Black
Author Photo Credit: Ryan Powell

Twitter: wordeeeupdates
Facebook: facebook.com/wordeee/
E-mail: contact@wordeee.com
Published by Wordeee Beacon, NY
Website: www.wordeee.com
Printed in the USA

CONTENTS

1981: "Wonderful! What can I say but wonderful? Yes, it's wonderful. Tonight has been
so wonderful and new. And I couldn't have
done it alone, I thank you."

—Deena Jones Press Conference from
Dreamgirls.

2022: "To anyone who has ever—ever—had a dream, and thought your dream shouldn't, wouldn't, couldn't come true, I'm here to tell you that this is what believing looks like."

—My Emmy Award Speech

DEDICATION

This book is dedicated to you Dear Reader. There are many books you could've chosen but you chose this one. Maybe it was the cover, maybe it was your interest in me and my story. Whatever the reason, I thank you for choosing my book because it was written for you, to encourage you, to inspire you to help you discover just how important you and your life journey really are. So, grab your favorite beverage, settle in, and get ready to drink from my wisdom well because this book is dedicated to you, Dear Reader.

AUTHOR'S NOTE

It's important to note that to me, DIVA is more than big hair and attitude. DIVA is an acronym for Divinely Inspired Victoriously Alive/Aware/Awesome, and if it were Sunday, Anointed! A DIVA is Definitely Inspirational and Vivaciously Alive. And DIVAs are Daringly Inquisitive and Valiantly Aware. So, my DIVAs in training, create your own magnificent DIVA and embrace her or him fearlessly. You will never know the DIVA you are to become until you do. And when you finally get there, you'll laugh out loud and dance in step with your DIVA self, knowing that you, too, are Divinely Inspired, Victoriously Alive. So, go on! Be inwardly gorgeous and outwardly fabulous. DIVA!

INTRODUCTION

HOW I BECAME A DIVA

I am the ultimate DIVA, at least that's what they tell me. I have been called DIVA on TV shows, podcasts, radio shows, and in magazines. I have been called DIVA by close friends and utter strangers. I have been called every kind of DIVA you can imagine, from renaissance DIVA to warrior DIVA, real-life DIVA to queen DIVA, and my favorite, DIVA-licious. I've heard it more times than I can count. Sheryl Lee Ralph is a true DIVA. And to them I say, "Thank you!"

Being called a DIVA used to bother me a lot. People loved to throw around the "D" word and most times it's synonymous with the "B" word. Whether you spell witch with a "W" or a "B," that is not me.

When most people hear the word "DIVA" in describing someone, the first thing that pops into their mind is a selfish, rude person with big, no; bigger, badder, nastier attitude! And there certainly are DIVAs who fit that bill. You know them. The A-list celebrity who finds their collection of Louis Vuitton luggage stacked in the wrong order. They pitch a fit, throw their cell phone at the nearest passerby, end up in court *and* on the cover of *People* magazine.

"What a DIVA!" says the press.

Then there's the young actress, in her first film, who refuses to leave her trailer, because Craft Services forgot to stock her favorite brand of bottled water and golden M&Ms. She was not playing the role of DIVA and it's obvious she has been painfully miscast. She holds up filming for three hours and when she finally gets to the set, she doesn't know her lines! Yet, there are no consequences for her when she's offered the film's sequel and her own reality show—'DIVA' in training? Not in my book.

And then there is the wannabe DIVA. You probably know a few of those DIVAs yourself. They aren't easy to miss. They're usually loud and rude, with a touch of violence thrown in for bad measure. The wannabe DIVA wouldn't hesitate to steal your parking spot, your man or woman, and she'll go for it all without so much as an "I'm sorry," or "Excuse me." You can love them or hate them, and it won't make a bit of difference because the only thing they think about is themselves.

DIVAs, according to public perception, are egotistical, self-centered, high maintenance, spoiled little brats. However, here is the truth, my friends. None of the aforementioned people are true DIVAs. These people give DIVA a bad name. A real DIVA, the kind who makes you sit up and take notice in a good way, is a person of strength, character, and has a beauty that radiates from within. He copies no one. She is her own woman. Now that's my kind of DIVA.

Our kind of DIVA has a voice and uses it to speak her mind, while understanding that inner thoughts do not always need to be outer thoughts. Our DIVA loves themselves; believes in themself enough to respect themself and others. Would a true DIVA disrespect themself and others by pitching hissy fits, fighting, cursing, shooting off guns and throwing things at people? NO! Not our DIVA. A true DIVA would never waste their time, or stoop to the lows of acting like a petty, nasty "B" word. A real DIVA gets what they want because people want to give it to them, and a real DIVA earns respect by respecting themselves and others.

So, when, and why did the term "DIVA" turn into such an insult? To find the answer, you have to take a look into the past, because any DIVA worth their salt pays respect to their legacy. Some believe the term "DIVA" originated from opera over two centuries ago. DIVA was used to describe the classic, self-centered, prima donna, storming off the stage with a cry of, "Call me when you get it together!" These women were notorious for creating chaos and confusion. They lived for drama and would have frightened the daylights out of the likes of a little wannabe DIVA. And, they wouldn't have to say a word to do it.

When digging deeper however, to discover the origins of DIVA, you'll find that the word became part of the English language in the late 19th century to describe a woman of extraordinary gifts and talent. The word "DIVA" comes from the Italian noun for female deity, which is derived from the Latin word *divus, a*nd "DIVA "translates to goddess. That's right! At her very roots, the DIVA is a goddess. Of course, she is! A DIVA is divine. She is, after all, a goddess! A DIVA is nothing if not inspiring. A DIVA is victorious. A DIVA is anointed. She is a chosen woman. A DIVA looks into the mirror and loves what she sees. She knows that she has to take care of that woman staring back at her, and she knows the truth: If you don't love yourself, how in the world are you going to love anyone else. My kind of DIVA is woman enough to love herself to the core of her being.

Those women and a few men too, cussing, fussing, shooting, and fighting anyone who dares to look at them sideways are fakes, phonies, and pure imposters. My kind of DIVA has better things to do, like improve themself and their community. She respects herself and those around her. He is a role model. And he owns it, because he knows he no longer has the freedom to ignore the impact he has on generations to come. Children are definitely watching, and my kind of DIVA is changing the world in big and small ways. And, yes! We look good doing it.

I never did set out to be divine or inspiring. I never knew that I would be cast in the role of DIVA. I believe that I am the accidental DIVA, but not really, because I am a woman with deep respect for myself and for others. RESPECT! Nevertheless, when people come up and tell me how I inspired them to own their talent and strengths; well, I say, "If that's the kind of DIVA woman you see me as, then I'm all right with that."

I am often asked how I became a DIVA. Well, I had good teachers. All DIVAs have a DIVA-mentor or an auntie in her head who shepherded her into DIVA-land. And if you don't have one, you need to search one out. I had many DIVA mentors in my head growing up Diahann Carroll—so beautiful. Miriam Makeba—a singer and revolutionary from South Africa; Yvonne Brathwaite Burke—ground-breaking politician and mother; Diana Ross and every single one of the Supremes. I mean, I secretly wanted to grow up and dye my hair "Mary-Wilson-blonde!" And then there was Nina Simone, a conscious and transformative DIVA.

Nina Simone was a bold soul sister; and there was nothing conventional about her. She was a real rule breaker, and what I call an obviously Black woman. You see, if you are two shades darker than Halle Berry, a lot of people might say that you are too dark or too black. Ms. Nina Simone was at least four shades darker than Halle Berry, living in a time when many people considered Black anything but beautiful. Nina Simone came to own her DIVA moment when her dear friend, playwright and political activist, Lorraine Hansberry died.

Nina, in that sad but freeing DIVA moment, yanked off her wig and wrote the song, "To Be Young,

Gifted, and Black." I remember hearing that song on the radio, and something changed for me and for so many of my generation. That song helped usher in a new kind of awareness when Black pride was on the rise. Much like the reaction of so many young, Black people today seeing Beyoncé's visual album, *Black is King*, "To Be Young, Gifted, and Black "evoked a new level of pride. Just as DIVA Nina had been changed by Lorraine Hansberry, many are elevating their consciousness through Beyoncé's music. Like Nina, Beyoncé recreated herself as the DIVA Black woman she is.

I was empowered by Nina, and I was changed. I had seen earlier pictures of Nina Simone posing in those old, too tight gowns and flashing straight wigs, the kind Negro women of that time wore, because through the eyes of the world, their natural hair was unacceptable. Thank God for her crowning act when DIVA Nina snatched off that wig and took to the stage. When she sang, "To Be Young, Gifted, and Black," or "Mississippi Goddam," she was making a real statement with her bold jewelry, African kaftans, and her short Afro. She looked so powerful and comfortable in her Black skin—her Black and beautiful skin. It was as if she were saying, "I am who I am, and there is nothing wrong with me. I am Black. I am Beautiful. I am Gifted and I am Proud. There is no reason for me to hide anything about myself, not even my natural hair. Ms. Simone was one of the first Black female artists to go natural, along with Aretha Franklin and Roberta Flack. And that summer, much to the shock of my parents, so did I and a host of rising teenagers and college students. Subsequently, most of Black America embraced the Afro and it became an icon of being Black and Proud.

I was at one with Ms. Simone. Whenever she opened her mouth to share that gorgeous voice of hers, she'd wail and moan, singing those songs of protest, and in turn finding her own kind of peace. She sang them in a way that made you say, "That is a proud Black woman right there—an African woman. And that woman is a beautiful "DIVA!" What an impression she made on me.

I believe that God orders your steps from the day you are born and with a little faith, mountains are scaled. He or She had ordered my steps to the South of France to attend a dinner honoring Gregory Peck, during the Cannes Film Festival. I took my seat in the lavishly decorated room with its motif of white flowers and candles and a table set for royalty. When I looked up, sitting right in front of me was the DIVA Ms. Nina Simone. She was older then and in a wheelchair. She was still as beautiful as ever with that lovely Black skin that refused to crack. I immediately got up from my seat and walked over to her.

"Excuse me," I said, "but you're Nina Simone."

She looked at me with a huge wide smile and proudly said, "Yes, I am!"

She was wearing a turban, pearls, and a vibrant, golden yellow silk gown. She was charming and still outspoken. We talked briefly about *Dreamgirls* and shared mutual moments of adoration. I could hardly believe I was talking to her.

Her story is known to the world. Yes, she did have controversy in her life. Utter her name and the likelihood is you'll get the story about how she carried a small pistol in her purse and wasn't afraid to pull it out. Like all of us, she had failures and a few broken hearts. But like any true DIVA, she was never one to lie down and roll over during hard times. She had learned that mistakes often turn into great successes. True DIVAs never just survive—they thrive!

When Nina Simone said she was proud of me, she had no idea what she was doing for the little girl she'd inspired to cut off her hair, to put gloss on her full lips, and say to the world, "This is who I am!"

The DIVA I am today exist because the fearless women who came before me would not let the world define them. And that is why I am writing this book, because of DIVAs like Nina Simone, Grandma Becky, Nana, Mrs. Lil Brown, Auntie Carolyn, Auntie Nae, Rosalind Cash, Virginia Capers, Josephine Premice, Beverly Manley, Pat Ramsey, Winsome Bryant, Nancy Wilson, Susan Taylor, and of course, my mother, T.H. Ivy Ralph, OD (Order of Distinction) who led the way in self-definition and determination. They were all the kinds of women I wanted to be strong, proud, and full of purpose. They fought the odds and just kept going. They inspired me just by being themselves and by loving me.

I hope after you finish reading this book, you, too, will be inspired. I hope that when someone calls you "DIVA," you lift your head, open your heart, and respond, "Thank you!"

CHAPTER ONE

A STAR IS BORN

"When Broadway history is being made, you can feel it," read *The New York Times*, headline on December 21, 1981. And that was just the beginning.

That was the review I woke up to that wintery morning in New York, after the opening night performance of *Dreamgirls* on Broadway. It had been a long, rough road. However, that single review opened the floodgates of fame. There would be television appearances and Tony nominations. My picture would grace the pages of *Vogue, Bazaar, Glamour, Essence*, and the now iconic cover of *Ebony* magazine. People would offer body parts to be signed; and most of them I signed with a smile. The tiny dressing room I shared with sweet Loretta Devine would overflow with flowers, telegrams, and gifts: My first Louis Vuitton bag—a gift from a drag queen; a vertical record player from Rick James; a bottle of perfume sent from Diane Von Furstenberg; backstage visits from Sylvester Stallone, Michael Jackson, Luther Vandross. Ah, people I had only heard on the radio or seen from the seat of my local movie theater. Overnight, I had gone from being just another struggling actress, pounding the pavement with a movie and a few TV shows under my belt, to being loved and adored by perfect strangers in the theater and on the streets of New York.

Night after night, the audiences rose to their feet and showered us with the kind of applause that let you know that you are loved—really, truly loved! God, it felt good.

Overnight, along with my cast mates, I had become the toast of the town, the *belle* of the ball on Broadway, and my life would be forever changed. If you had told me what was in store, I would have never believed it. If you would have told me that decades later there would be a *Dreamgirls* movie with a great, young star cast in the role I had created, singing songs, and saying lines I helped write, or that anyone would ever associate my name with a word like "DIVA" in the same way they did Ms. Ross, Ms. Diana Ross! Well...ha-ha!, I would have thought you were just plain crazy. *Dreamgirls* was a miracle on Broadway, and no less so in my life.

Had I only known, and had not been a young novice, I would never have signed away my creative rights to *Dreamgirls* for a single U.S. dollar. I was young, dumb, and loving the job I was doing, and the business of the business never crossed my mind. I was living my dream, stepping out under those bright lights every night, singing my heart out, and looking good! After all, I was only twenty-three years old, about to turn twenty-four.

My mother also faced some of her greatest challenges at the age of 24. That was the year she came to the United States with the dream of getting a job, going to school to become a nurse, and buying a house. "Don't let life frighten you," my mother would say in her melodious Jamaican accent, seeding in me what I did not understand then as fearlessness.

Travel back then was complicated, and as a foreigner seeking to move to the U.S., someone had to "sponsor" you, which meant they had to show the financial where-withal to be able to support you. The United States was clear and non-negotiable on not having immigrants become a financial burden on their social system.

It was a long and expensive trip from Jamaica. Because of the cost, most island immigrants flew to Miami and then took the train to New York. My moth-er's Aunt Maude had sent for her, and she was expect-ing to get her money back. My mother found work in Harlem Hospital as a nurse's aide so she could repay Aunt Maude and get a jump start on learning about her future career. As long as she lived, my mother never liked to owe anybody anything, especially money.

Mommy enrolled in night school to further her dream of an education but dropped out after only three weeks in America, when she met my father. He was a student at New York University (NYU), study-ing for his master's, and working nights as a hospital operator. My mother said that the very first time she heard his voice over the loudspeaker she just had to meet him. And that was that.

What makes this story even more special is that dur-ing that time in the 1950s, there was a separation between Black Americans and West Indians. American Blacks used to call West Indians, "monkey chasers," "coconut," and other vicious names, the groups therefore stayed to themselves. But not my mother. She heard that American voice, and she was going to meet him and introduce herself to him. Her life would be forever changed by not being afraid of rejection, or anything else. It's sad to think about there being West Indian dreams and an American reality. But that was how it was.

My grandmother on my father's side, Julia Ward, was born in the summer of 1910 in North Carolina. She was never frightened by life. Nana never let anyone tell her what she could or could not do. As a young girl, she was considered one of the most beautiful girls in her small, dusty, North Carolina town. Like any of the young ladies of that time, she could cook, sew, and was active in her church. After Sunday dinner, she would sit crocheting on the front porch with her sisters and mother. Young men would pass in the distance, since the house was set far back off of the road, and tip their hats, hoping for some sort of acknowledgement. These belles would barely acknowledge their many suitors.

"If I liked one," Nana used to tell me, "I might give 'em a tiny nod, but never a wave. You would never yell, 'hello,' or offer any conversation. That just wasn't lady-like. Besides, you never talked to any young man you hadn't been formally introduced to."

My grandmother helped teach me the value of politeness. She believed that manners really mattered, especially for a pretty Negro. With real manners, she could be respected. Nana also taught me that you could be a lady and still have your own mind. In her time, most believed marriage was a woman's only option for financial stability. My grandmother never let anyone tell her what to believe. She had her own thoughts and beliefs.

With her rare beauty my grandmother had caught the attention of a rather fancy man in her town. She was not thrilled. Most women would have welcomed the attention, but not my grandmother. She didn't like it. She didn't like him, much less love him. And beyond that, she wanted more for herself. She had read somewhere about factories up North looking to hire Negro workers. Unemployed Negroes would gather at certain parts of town and were offered bus tickets and train tickets to work in factory cities, such as Chicago, New York, and Detroit. This was the beginning of The Great Migration. Being a true old school DIVA herself, my grandmother who was one of thirteen brothers and sisters, decided there was more out there in the world to explore. So, without telling anyone, she accepted a one-way bus ticket, packed her bags full of dreams and headed North. My grandmother was a true DIVA in the best sense of the word.

Eventually, my grandmother married. Her husband wasn't the richest man, but my grandfather was a quiet man, a family man, a great sportsman, hunter, athlete, and above all, a good man. He loved taking me to the dog shows and tennis matches. He was a talented golfer, but never got the chance to enjoy the fairways simply because of the color of his skin. He would caddy for white men to get the chance to play a few rounds himself. And he could fix anything, including people.

With the support of a good woman—and any real DIVA woman inspires her partner to be the best they can be—they set out to make a life together. And it was a good life.

My grandfather, socially minded, went on to help countless young people in their community. He developed an after-school tennis program for students to keep the neighborhood children out of harm's way, as he felt an idle mind was the devil's workshop, and he was right. In the end, my grandfather was murdered in our family home by intruders. The irony: the young man who committed the crime was a part of the athletic program Gramps created for young people in need of an outlet. My grandmother stood beside my grandfather right up until the end. Much later in her life she finally told me about that night.

"He just bled-out," she said. "I tried to hold the blood back, but his insides were scrambled. I tried to hold the blood back, hold his insides together, but it was too late. I screamed, but it was like no one could hear me, like there was a veil over us and the house. I held him and I just watched life leave him. Then, he was gone."

Now there was some discrepancy in my mind about the real story from what I'd thought. My grandmother told me it was a crisp Wednesday evening in September when the boys came to rob the house. Wednesday was Bible Study, so they figured everyone would be at church. They expected to find an empty home. However, that night my grandparents had left church early to have dinner with some friends. Arriving home, my grandmother saw the back door open and entered the house. There were intruders. She grabbed a kitchen knife and went after the thieves. My grandmother was a fighter and she lunged for one of the boys. Before the knife could reach him, my grandfather had been shot with a double-barrel shotgun, point blank to the chest.

I often wondered what would have happened if my grandmother had not gone after that boy. But that wasn't her way. Like any real DIVA of her time and now, my grandmother stayed true to herself and so she would go to any lengths to protect those she loved, even if it meant putting herself in danger—even if it killed her.

When I was younger, I often wondered too, "What was she thinking at that moment?" Now, I think I know. Not only was she defending her husband, but she was also defending herself, her children, the life she loved, and all of the years she had struggled to make a comfortable home for her family, putting three children through college and one through the Air Force.

Nana survived, but she too had been shot. Julia, one of the most beautiful women in her North Carolina town, was shot right in the face. She was scarred forever, both physically and emotionally. However, she did what she had to do and passed that strength on to me. I had always been told that I was very much like her. And for that, I'm forever grateful.

Like my mother, she passed her fearlessness on to me. A lifetime later, that same fearlessness gave me the guts to find my way to Hollywood.

I remember calling my father from a phone booth at the Los Angeles airport. I had not even collected my luggage. I just found the nearest phone booth and called, "Daddy," I said.

"Sheryl Lee Ralph," he said, using all three of my names in a way that let me know that I was in trouble. "Where are you?

"California."

"What are you doing in California?" he asked, completely dumbfounded.

I didn't have an answer because I wasn't sure myself. I had just landed in the United States, after completing a tour of duty with the Department of Defense. With a government-issued rank of GS12, I was the singing bodyguard for the 1975 Penthouse Pet of the Year: Anneka Di Lorenzo. I will never forget all of the servicemen holding up their open *Penthouse* magazine asking, "Which one are you?"

I was only nineteen and still a bit on the innocent side. Embarrassed as I was, I had to tell them that I was only there to sing. Some were disappointed because they knew what they wanted to see, and others were all smiles after hearing my voice. One man, I'll never forget him, simply looked at me and said, "I'm glad you're not in the magazine."

Performances for the Armed Forces were some of the best times in my life. To this day, I have a great fondness for those who serve our country. It is a great sacrifice. Now, they could be a tough audience to please, but in the end, they always love you for just showing up for them. And it was a great experience for a DIVA in training. Because for our servicemen, I had the opportunity to travel halfway around the world, seeing places and things many people could only imagine seeing. Uncle Sam took very good care of me.

After my tour of duty was over, I had to return to New York with a stopover in San Francisco or Los Angeles. I didn't have to think twice. I chose L.A., the City of Angels. So, there I was at LAX Airport, a nineteen-year old, fresh out of college, trying to be a singer/actress. Obviously not worldly or savvy enough, yet here I was, a young girl who'd gotten off the plane, left her luggage behind, and headed to the nearest payphone to call home because she had no idea where to go or how to achieve her dreams. My father was not thrilled.

"You'd better get back on that plane and come home! Come home now!"

"Daddy, you know I'm coming home, but not yet. Right now, I have to be here."

"What in heaven's name are you going to do there?"

"I don't know yet."

My father sighed. He knew firsthand just how stubborn I could be when I made up my mind about something. I just knew my future was in L.A. and that I was going to be a star. All of the soldiers had told me that, and I knew it. What I didn't know was where I would be sleeping that night.

"Well," said my father, knowing I couldn't be convinced otherwise. Deep down I knew he was cheering me on, despite my mother's insistence I find a more predictable profession. I often wondered if I reminded daddy of his dream deferred. Whatever it was, he was always there to remind me that it was my life and my dream, no matter what my mother said.

"Believe it or not, I just hung up the phone with my cousin Mable," Daddy continued. "I haven't spoken to her in years, and just like that she happened to call me long distance today."

"Cousin Mable."

"Yes, Mable. And you will never believe where she lives!"

Like my mother and grandmother, I was not afraid to take the risk. That's another important lesson I learned from them. Any Divinely Inspired, Victorious Alive woman takes risks. Yes. You are bound to make mistakes, but a "mistake" is simply another word for experience. Enough experiences often add up to success.

Years later, I would love watching reruns of the TV show, *Julia*. Seeing my grandmother's name splashed across the TV screen brought back memories of her fortitude. One of the middle names I gave my daughter is Julia, in honor of my grandmother. I hope this is a reminder of the current of strength running through our lineage and veins.

Nana was proud of my being on Broadway. She had always dreamed of singing and dancing on stage like Josephine Baker, Florence Mills, or Bessie Smith. Sadly, back then that wasn't the kind of career a real lady pursued if she had other options. Showing your legs much less your cleavage was socially unacceptable, and certainly unladylike. Everybody believed that the life of a show girl could lead to tragedy. The use of drugs and alcohol were common and still is. So, my grandmother chose marriage and kept her singing to the church choir. But she'd, no doubt, passed that artsy gene on to my father who then passed it on to me. I finally manifested it for us all.

Nana changed gradually after the shooting. Sometimes she would be cheerful, sipping her favorite scotch. And sometimes she would seem distant and somewhere far away. During my run on Broadway in *Dreamgirls*, I would often call my grandmother before the show. Nothing made her happier than those calls from the theater.

"Who was in the audience? Who had I met? Was I eating to keep up my strength? "Because you have to be strong to be really famous," she would say.

And before signing off, her requests never changed: "Sing a little song for me, Sheryl Lee, sing a little song for me."

Wow! Was she right about everything, and believe me, I sang a little song for her.

I'm still singing for my grandmother. Every time I open my mouth, whether on a Broadway stage, or for my husband and children, I sing for her. I sing for my mother and all the strong women who came before me, who shaped me into the woman I am and still becoming today. These are my DIVA mentors and the women I look to for strength when I feel as though the weight of my world is too much to carry.

I was blessed to have a wonderful mother and grandmother: Two women different as night and day.

They both loved me deeply and unconditionally, strengthening me with life lessons that continue to guide me. But they weren't the only ones who inspired me and gave me wings.

When I was about 10 years old, I met Susan Taylor while on summer vacation in Jamaica. She would later chart a stellar life becoming the Editor-in-Chief of *Essence Magazine*. My mother by now had long found her way into entrepreneurship, and her design salon, The House of Ivy, kept me in contact with the who's who of visitors to the island. My mom's friend, Pat Ramsey, and her brilliant photographer husband, Ken, knew this young, vibrant model at the time so naturally when she was visiting the island, they took her to meet my mother. I remember the first time I saw her. She was bald headed, with big eyes, and huge hoop earrings. I was as smitten, as any little girl would be when she comes face-to-face with a beautiful big girl glowing with confidence from every pore. There is an iconic picture of Susan Taylor taken by Mr. Ramsey in which she is looking over her shoulder. In my young mind, every time I look at the picture, I imagine her looking right at me and saying, "You coming?" I have followed Susan Taylor to some degree my whole life and career, emulating her grace and kindness. She is a Queen DIVA.

At the age of fifteen, during another summer in Jamaica, I met Rosalind "Roz" Cash, whom I knew to be a great actress. Roz took me under her wing and encouraged my dreams. Originally from New Jersey, she sometimes visited me at Rutgers University and always caused a stir with her handsome companion and green Mercedes. She encouraged my education in school and on stage. She helped me in securing my audition for the Negro Ensemble Company's Actor Training Program and was so proud of my acceptance to the program. She opened her home to me when I needed a place to stay in Los Angeles and remained supportive of me up until her untimely death due to cancer.

I met Virginia Capers at the age of nineteen, when I was chosen as one of The Top 10 College Women in America by *Glamour* magazine. With that award, I would join an elite group of women, which included Martha Stewart. The greatest gift I was given with that award was the opportunity to meet a woman of influence in my chosen field. I chose to meet Tony Award winner for *Raisin*, the musical version of A *Raisin in the Sun*, aunt Virginia Capers. The actress immediately embraced me like her own child. She helped me set goals and deadlines in my career and encouraged me as I crossed every finish line. She sat front and center when I performed in community theater. She was there for the premiere of *A Piece of the Action* and *Dreamgirls* and was as proud of me as any mother would be when I was nominated for the Tony Award. She told me she wasn't surprised.

Aunt Virginia made sure my first apartment was suitable by finding it herself. She always shared her showbiz war stories, and always encouraged me to take a higher road. According to her, "the same ass you kicked today, you may have to kiss tomorrow!" I keep her picture at my front door, so she will always see my comings and goings. I miss her and love her, and I thank her.

Elizabeth Taylor, who I did not know as long, or as well, was a wealth of support as I branched out speaking about AIDS through my DIVA Foundation. Founded in 1990, I wanted to memorialize the many friends lost to the AIDS epidemic. Another quick-witted woman, Ms. Taylor told me not to be disheartened by those who tried to bring me down. "Don't let those people stop you," she said. "Most of them couldn't find their ass if it wasn't connected to them."

These women made a deep and unforgettable mark on my life as a woman and a performer.

Unfortunately, we are not all blessed that way. Perhaps your mother was unavailable. Maybe she had life issues or wasn't around much or you never met her in the first place. Does that mean you won't have your own DIVA mentor? A real DIVA in training won't let that stop her. Find your role model and seek their mentorship.

I owe so much to these women and believe me, there are women out there who will do the same for you. A real DIVA finds her DIVA mentors. She seeks them out. A real DIVA, the kind you want to be, looks to the women who came before to inspire her. So, next time you feel overwhelmed and think you have nowhere to turn, remember the women who paved the way for you. Search for the DIVA around you. Maybe you know her personally in your church, or at your school. Maybe you've heard her on the radio. Maybe she's your local politician or entrepreneur. Maybe you've only read about her in books and magazines or read about her online. The celebrity or actress, they all have lessons to teach you. Just as my grandmother and mother gave me strength, your DIVA mentor can do the same for you. With the right DIVA mentor, you will find a wise and trusted guide and advisor—a woman who serves as a role model just by living. Look to her for guidance and you will not believe the heights to which you will rise.

I have been blessed with the support and mentorship of some of the most wonderful and giving women God ever created. Some of these women found me. Others I sought out on my own. You never know when a DIVA mentor will come into your life. So, keep your eyes open for her arrival.

▼

DIVA Lesson One
Find Your Role Model and
Seek Their Mentorship.

CHAPTER TWO

FINDING ME

When I was growing up, my mother always used to tell me in her lilting Jamaican accent, "Be a doctor. Be a lawyer. And if you can't do that then marry one!"

I knew better than to argue with a strong West Indian woman once she had made up her mind about what I should be doing with my life. No matter what I said, I knew my mother only wanted what she felt was best for me. I had parents who did their best when it came to loving me. They made sure I had a good education. Even more, they made sure I felt good about myself, no matter how funny looking I was. And I was truly funny looking. That self-esteem my parents built inside of me is what kept me from being afraid when at sixteen years old, I entered my freshman year of college at Rutgers University—in its first class that accepted women.

Rutgers had historically been a male university. And with time, when greater minds prevailed, it opened its doors to women. In that inaugural year of women, only two African Americans were in that class. Of all the women and men accepted that year, I was the youngest.

Looking back, I should have been terrified. I should have had a million doubts in my mind. *What will they think of me? Will I fit in? Will I be able to handle the course load?* I wasn't frightened or nervous. After all, I was just sixteen. I was more excited to be there, and I never doubted that I belonged at that illustrious institution. My parents had taught me the value of hard work and I'd worked hard to get there, so I knew I had earned my place there, just like the great Paul Robeson. Besides, I had goals in life, and I was determined to meet them. If anyone ever thought I didn't belong, well, I didn't notice, and it wasn't any of my business. I was determined to succeed, and I wanted to make up my mind for myself in this world. I wanted to be a successful, respected doctor. That was the only part that didn't feel quite right. Still, my mother's voice rang loud and clear. Be a doctor! Be a lawyer! And if you can't do that, then marry one!!

I knew I could perform. I had been singing, dancing, and acting since I was a child. My talents *are* singing and acting. Those were things I knew I could do well. The year before I entered college, I had participated in the Miss Black Teenage America Pageant in New York. I wasn't dreaming about the Golden Statue and the Sparkling Crown, as much as I was dreaming about that scholarship check they gave the winner. I sang and danced my way to runner-up.

Even after taking home the first runner-up title and a $5,000 scholarship, which to my father's delight, paid for almost two years of college; it never occurred to me that I could sing and dance for a living, so I was at Rutgers as a pre-med student. I had no idea about destiny when I started at Rutgers. I had other things to think about, like a packed class schedule. Of course, a true DIVA can't escape her destiny because deep inside she knows who she is.

I will never forget my first day in one of my premed classes, I was presented with a hare (yes, h-a-r-e) and a scalpel. There was a dead bunny rabbit in front of me that I was expected to slice open with a sharp and shiny new little knife. "I don't think so!" I gave that scalpel back to the instructor and told him that this was the first and last time he would see Sheryl Lee Ralph. I left that class knowing I was never going to be a doctor, and immediately went over to the Registrar's Office to see if I could find a course that would help me become a lawyer.

Constitutional Law essentially encompasses all the foundational laws that our country is based upon. And that is a lot of laws. I sat in that class, and I was miserable. The teacher who taught that class was a small, tightly wound-up woman with glasses and a severe bun. She never smiled. Her speech was like chalk, screeching on the blackboard. And then there was real chalk screeching. I had to get out of there too. I'd left that class, with the same quickness, I left the other one.

So, there I was walking across the campus after leaving Constitutional Law class. It was a drab, gray day, and I felt drab and gray, too. Little Sheryl Lee Ralph, college girl, who had found freedom wearing her Afro, jeans and gold platform shoes, and textbooks loaded into her sharp African textile book bag. You see me! But in that moment I was having a complete and utter meltdown! Within my first month in college, it was clear I was not going to be able to live up to my mother's dream of becoming a doctor or a lawyer. And I wasn't even thinking about marrying one any time soon.

Back in the day, many women went to college to find their husbands. Many of my good friends met their future spouses while at Rutgers. However, I knew that early marriage wasn't for me either. I was younger than my classmates and the idea of finding a husband, starting a family, and giving up my dreams—THERE WAS NO WAY! Just like my grandmother, I knew my own dreams had to come first. The only problem: I just wasn't sure what those dreams were yet.

I wandered through the campus thinking, *"How was I going to tell my mother?"* The thought of her reaction to my revelation filled me with dread. I did not want to hear her mouth after I broke the news. Somehow as I wandered campus, I ended up in front of the theater. Fate? Maybe. My subconscious leading me there? More likely. And there, hanging on the front door of the theater was a sign:

"Auditions Today."

I didn't think twice. I knew the world was full of excitement and inspiration and I knew I wasn't going to find either of those things in Organic Chemistry, Biology or Constitutional Law. I was not going to become a doctor or a lawyer. The thought that crossed my mind was, how could I possibly tell my mother? But, I'd have to worry about that later. I practically flew into the auditorium and signed up to audition. I had memorized my monologue and song from the Miss Black Teenage America Pageant, and I was ready to use them.

Dr. John Bettenbender was an older, rumpled looking man with a long white beard, and he smoked a pipe. He was the head King, really, of the theater department. Everyone knew it except me. He looked up from his seat, surrounded by a large cloud of smoke and grumbled.

"Who are you?"

"Sheryl Ralph," I said. "And I would like to audition."

Grumble-grumble. "Well," he said, looking at me over his glasses. "Get on the stage then."

I dropped my bag of legal textbooks and was on the stage so fast, I made my own head spin. I had no idea what I was doing, but the moment I took my place center stage, I'd found my home. Whatever I was doing felt so good and so right.

Dr. Bettenbender just looked at me and kept smoking that pipe of his. I took a deep breath, opened my mouth, and performed my monologue, which I had written myself. I followed it up with an a capella version of "Summertime." Ah! That little speech and song had gotten me first runner up in the Miss Black Teenage America Pageant in New York, and it also got me the King's attention. After being confronted with having to cut up the Easter Bunny and sitting through that boring law class, and the realization that the worlds of medicine and law would not be mine; in that moment of auditioning, I felt completely alive, and I gave it my all. Right there on that stage, I felt whole. I had found myself! And I am so grateful for that.

When I finished my audition, Dr. Bettenbender was silent for quite a while, with that pipe plume of smoke circling his head. Finally, he opened his mouth.

Grumble-grumble. "What did you say your name was?"

"Sheryl Ralph...Sheryl Lee Ralph" I repeated, already trying on my celebrity name, which was really just my middle name.

"Well, Sheryl Lee Ralph," he said. "You just got yourself cast."

Just like that I could see my whole future spread out before me. I liked what I saw. My future was on the stage—not in the courtroom, and certainly not in the operating room. I felt utter relief.

I spent that year taking acting classes, meeting with other young actors, learning my craft, and looking forward to the new challenge each day would bring me. I began to see that this joy I had discovered, the ability to entertain, could actually become a career. My career. I might actually make money doing what I love. That thought filled me with pride and hope, not to mention fear. Yes. I was afraid. *"How could I do it, this acting thing? How would I survive?" "Most of all, what about my parents?"*

My parents loved me, adored me. They sacrificed to give me the gift of an exceptional education at one of the nation's leading universities and made sure there were always hands to lift me when I fell. How could I disappoint them? Not to mention, I wasn't exactly picking the most stable career path. All those things I was taught that good parents do for their children: Take them to church, keep them clothed and fed and safe was up for grabs. Would I be able to do that for my future children if I had any as an entertainer? There was the belief that all actresses worried about was keeping their bodies and minds in shape and their lives free from the entanglement of other people. My mind was a mess of conflicting emotions because in my mind I knew one day I was going to be somebody's mother and maybe my body would no longer be the same. Then I would go on stage, and everything made sense.

I found my joy on the stage. In fact, center stage is my home. By the end of my freshman year, I had been invited to compete in the Irene Ryan Scholarship Competition, as part of the American College Theater Festival. The Irene Ryan Foundation awards scholarships to outstanding student performers. Irene Ryan, known to millions of television viewers as the feisty pipe-smoking, moonshine making granny in the hit comedy series *The Beverly Hillbillies*. After a decade long career, she made her Broadway debut in the musical *Pippin* appearing as an aging swinger with a song for which she was nominated for a Tony. Unfortunately, the incomparable Irene Ryan had a stroke centerstage after making her entrance and passed on soon after.

College Theater departments from around the country nominate their top students to compete, and hundreds of talented young actors and actresses practice for months in eligible college theater productions, hoping to bring top honors to their colleges and universities.

I was shocked to find out that I had been chosen to compete. Dr. Bettenbender couldn't have been happier. I was picked based upon a performance in a play he had directed, written by a promising student playwright, by the name of Neil Cuthbert also at Rutgers. Neil would go on to write the notable movies, *Hocus Pocus* and *The Adventures of Pluto Nash*. The play was called "The Soft Touch." Without regard to color, Dr. Bettenbender cast who he felt was the best actress for the lead. And the American College Theater Festival obviously agreed. He was like a proud father.

Freshmen were not usually chosen to compete, and I had only been seriously studying theater for a year. The odds were against me, but I didn't even think about that. I just felt honored, and I figured I would be getting great practice. To everyone's surprise, I won the regional competition and was invited to perform in Washington, D.C., at the Kennedy Center for the national title.

I do not remember if I felt nervous or out of place that day. I might have been, but once I stepped onto the stage of the Kennedy Center, I was once again home. I was center stage where all of the worries in the world melted away. At the moment, I was doing what I was born to do. I was sharing the gifts God had given me with a welcoming audience. I was loving it. At the end of my performance, the audience exploded with applause. My mother and father were so happy. My grandmother just beamed with the kind of pride words cannot explain. I took my seat with my family and extended family, who had traveled great distances just to see me on that stage. My mother seemed at the moment to have forgotten I was to be a doctor or a lawyer, but she had not.

We watched the other students perform and waited anxiously for the results. Then, the moment of truth. Greg Morris, who starred in the TV series, *Mission Impossible*, one of the first Black actors to ever star in a hit TV series was one of the judges. I was so happy just to be on the same stage with him. Later in my career I would share the screen with his talented son, Greg, and daughter Iona. I was happy and content. The biggest surprise of all—I won! They said my name out loud, "Sheryl Lee Ralph." I couldn't believe it. Out of all the students in the country, they chose me!! I had to pinch myself. I knew in that moment no matter what I had to face at home, I had found my joy forever. And when you find your joy, your audience, whoever they may be—I mean from relatives to coworkers to whatever you believe in up above or not—they will all be applauding for you.

Between the American College Theater Festival Scholarship and the scholarship, I had received performing in the Miss Black Teenage American Pageant, I had made almost $10,000. Anyway, you looked at it, that was a nice chunk of money. Those were figures my father could stand behind.

"Honey," he said, with that great voice of his, "You act all you want. You go right on and do it. You act, Sheryl Lee Ralph."

My father was so happy I was acting my way through college. Acting was paying for my tuition, and he was delighted. But my mother, well, that was another story.

I often meet young women who hate their jobs. They don't like the people they work with, and they don't like what they do. Had I gone in another direction, I would be just like them: unhappy; making everyone around me unhappy and wondering why I can't find and keep a good relationship. Here's what I tell those women: If you are working at something and it isn't making you happy, well, you need to find yourself another job. If you don't find your work fulfilling, well, you need to find yourself another job. If you don't wake up in the morning with a feeling that you just can't wait to get to work and be the best you can possibly be, well you probably know what I'm going to say:

find yourself another job! If you take a job just to take a job, then you aren't really living. You are just surviving, not thriving.

Now don't get me wrong, sometimes a DIVA has to do what a DIVA has to do to put food on the table. And a DIVA doesn't hesitate when faced with those challenges. She knows to find her job at all costs because one day her real DIVA-self will arrive.

There are a million reasons and excuses to keep you from finding your joy and the work that fulfills you: The uncertainty of stepping out on faith alone; the fear of rejection; people telling you that it is impossible because it wasn't possible for them; others thinking you have lost your mind or are just plain crazy. This leads you to think *"What about the rent? What about my hair? My nails? My designer morning latte?"* All of those things cost money, honey. So, what are you going to do? Are you going to lie down and roll over with the daily unhappiness and say, "Well, I guess that's it?" Of course, you're not! You're a DIVA. And any real DIVA is willing to rise to the challenge of her own life. Catch it! A real DIVA is willing to rise to the challenge of her own life.

"Well, Ms. DIVA," you might be thinking, *"That's easy for you to say."* Listen. I didn't get where I am by taking the easy route. It hasn't been and wasn't easy for me, and it won't be for you. Life is hard, and then you die. Now when you get right down to it, you don't have any other choice except this one: follow your passion. The hardest part is the first step: Making the

choice to be happy. Living a happy life is a choice, and you are the one to make it. They say we make over 30,000 choices a day and on the day you choose joy, everything changes: your walk, your talk, the smile. Your choices all change because you are happy. A real DIVA knows that when she's happy, the world is a better place. A real DIVA knows that—once they find their joy.

It took quite a while, as in years, and the Tony nomination, and paying to rebuild her home in Jamaica before my mother would agree with Daddy. Who knows, I might have made an excellent lawyer and maybe even a better doctor if I'd been able to get over slicing up the Easter bunny but I for one will never know. And for that, I am very grateful.

▼

DIVA Lesson Two
Search for Your JOY Because When You Find It
and Are Doing What You Love to
Do Everything Will Be Alright.

CHAPTER THREE

I TOLD YOU SO

I had been through all those experiences that had pointed me to where I should be, and I knew I was in the right place. So, standing in that phone booth at the Los Angeles Airport, waiting for my father to call me back with the telephone number of the person who held my future in her hands seemed to take hours. As soon as I said, "I love you, Daddy," and promised him I would be careful and hung up, I put another dime in the pay phone.

His cousin, Mable, answered on the first ring. I would later find out that Mable always answered on the first ring because she was always near the phone. The phone, I would soon find out, was near the TV; the TV was near the window; and that, along with the packs of cigarettes she smoked daily, completed her world.

Most people thought Mable was happy to sit in the window, watching the action on the streets. The neighbors knew she hadn't been out in a long time, and they knew she wasn't about to come out. That she might be afraid of leaving—well, that thought never crossed their minds. I don't think anyone knew it at the time, but Mable suffered from severe depression. But even if they did, back then we didn't talk about "it." "It" was something you kept to yourself. We didn't know back then much about mental illness or its debilitating effects.

Mable had a lot on her plate already, just coping with day-to-day living. Now, she was about to get into something she could never have anticipated—a young Sheryl Lee Ralph, bubbling with enthusiasm and ready to take on the whole world. I was a nineteen-year-old girl, with one suitcase and it was filled with BIG dreams. Yes'm, Mable had no idea what she was in for.

Mable opened the door with a smile and welcomed me like a sunny day. She had made space for me in a small, back room. Looking back, it was about the size of one of my closets today. Yet, I could not have been happier. I did not waste time unpacking. I immediately got on the phone and started reaching out to the friends and few contacts I had within the entertainment industry. I also checked in with my answering service. It turned out that my acting teacher, Kris Keiser, from the Negro Ensemble Company, had been trying to track me down for weeks.

I called Kris back and learned that he was the Associate Producer on a new Sidney Poitier movie, and a role in the movie was perfect for me. Just like that! Before Mable had a chance to even figure out how long

I would be staying with her, I had gotten called in for an audition with Mr. Sidney Poitier! Me and Sidney! Sheryl Lee Ralph auditioning for *the* Sidney Poitier. The part was in, what would be, the last of the Sidney Poitier/Bill Cosby collaborations, *A Piece of the Action*. The film would be directed by Mr. Poitier himself. I was thrilled out of my mind. I figured it must be a sign, for real. Less than 24 hours in L.A., and I had an audition with an iconic, legendary, Oscar winner. I was exactly where I was meant to be. This first audition might lead to a part. A part might lead to a Hollywood career. Everything I had worked for, studied for, and dreamed about was right in front of me—ripe for the picking. It could all start with this one audition.

There was just one problem. I didn't have any way to get there. A nineteen-year-old was too young to rent a car in California plus I did not have a credit card. A taxi—well, that would have been way too expensive. And besides, where were the studios Warner Brothers anyway? My only option was to ask Cousin Mable to drive me there.

Well, to say that Mable freaked out would be putting it lightly. After hours of begging and soothing, she was still utterly panicked at the idea of driving anyone anywhere. She hadn't been behind a steering wheel in years. In the end, I somehow convinced her. I would like to believe it was a result of my powers of persuasion. Yet, the truth was simpler. The payoff for driving me to my audition, Cousin Mable would get to meet Sidney Poitier. For that, she would do something she hadn't done in years: Leave the safety of her TV and window world.

Of course, it was not easy. The drive from Mable's house in L.A. to the Warner Brothers Studio in the Valley should have taken maybe 30 minutes. Instead, it took Mable just about an hour and 30 minutes and a whole pack of cigarettes. The whole time I tried to stay calm and soothing, keeping up a steady stream of positivity. "You're doing it, Mable. We're almost there, Mable. See, isn't this fun? Can you believe we're going to meet Mr. Poitier?"

Inside, I wasn't feeling as calm. I realized this was very, very hard for Mable. She was pushing herself way past the comfort zone she'd lived in for so many years just to help me. In her own right Mable was a brave DIVA and she taught me another lesson: do it even if you don't want to. As the minutes ticked by and Mable eased her foot off the gas to light up another cigarette, after cigarette, after cigarette, I said silent prayers that we would even make it on time. Then just like that— you know, like in the movies—there it was looming before us, seeming to almost glow in the bright California sunshine: Warner Brothers Studio. "This is it!" I said, "California, here I am!"

Before I stepped into the room to meet with Mr. Poitier, I scoped out more information about the project than I knew what to do with. One such was who were the actresses going up against me for the part. My competition, well, the first one, was Tamu Blackwell. Tamu had just come off the movie *Claudine*, starring with one of my childhood inspirations, Diahann Carroll. Of course, I had seen Tamu's performance and I knew she was a talented actress. And if that wasn't enough, there was another talented actress reading for the role named Pamela—Pamela Poitier. Yes, Mr. Poitier's daughter. And then there was me—Little Sheryl Lee. I thought to myself: "Now, out of these three, who is not getting the role?" The answer was pretty clear to me.

In a moment like that, a lot of things run through one's head and that horrible question couldn't help but rear its ugly head. *What's the point?* I thought. Then I thought about Cousin Mable. After getting me to the studio, she was so exhausted and drenched with perspiration, she couldn't even come inside and get a glimpse of, let alone meet, her matinee idol. Nonetheless, she had found the strength to leave her house after all of those years just to be another angel in my life and start me on my way. That was a miracle, and I am forever grateful.

Getting there was a miracle within itself also. Maybe there were to be more miracles where that one came from for Cousin Mable and me. I had a lot of accountability riding on this audition. There was Cousin Mable, of course, to whom I owed a debt of gratitude; and my parents, who were probably sick with worry because I had decided to stay in Los Angeles after all. Then there was that nagging little voice saying, "What are you doing," which I tried to ignore and push away, and needed to silence but could never quite get rid of it.

I had chosen this route myself. I had to get myself together. I had to put my best self forward. I mean, I was lucky. I could have been well on my way to cutting open a cadaver at this point, so I had to do my very best to show the world that I had followed the direction of my passion and that I had made the right choice. Yes, I had something to prove.

Having something to prove can be a great motivator and I wanted something more than a great story to tell people about how I had once met Sidney Poitier. I wanted the part.

Sitting there with Tamu and Pamela, I decided there was no point in being intimidated. I was getting three minutes in the room to audition with an Oscar winner, and I was going to give it my best shot. Sometimes in this life, all you will get is three minutes. I certainly was not about to waste a second on second guessing.

The three minutes themselves were a blur. All I remember clearly was walking into this nice office, and there he was, Mr. Sidney Poitier. He immediately reminded me of my father. He was tall, and handsome, with a warm smile that made me feel comfortable right away. He shook my hand, and I fought off the urge to babble on about how much my mother loved him. My grandmother loved him. I loved him. I really fought the urge to tell him about how my dad, as he had told me many times, "I missed the opportunity to audition for his understudy in *A Raisin in the Sun*."

My dad had to make a serious choice in life, to be a father to his daughter and a husband to his wife or

43

chase his own dreams. My dad chose family. In the end, maybe that was why he was so supportive of my choice. This audition was for the both of us.

Everything Mr. Poitier did, from strolling across a room, to shaking the hand of an unknown actress, to accepting an Academy Award for Best Actor in "Lilies of the Field," is done with innate elegance. There is no way to describe him, except to say he was a true gentleman. From the way he carried himself and spoke in his everyday interactions, Mr. Poitier was a gentleman through and through.

I read the lines I had practiced and committed to memory. In his presence, I became a star in my head. I read that monologue as if I were an Oscar winner, too. I just remembered thinking, *That is Sidney Poitier, and he is really listening to me*! I was in the same room as *Ebony magazine* royalty, and I was giving that audition everything I had.

When I was done, Mr. Poitier smiled at me. "What's your name?" he said, his voice businesslike and utterly professional.

"Sheryl Lee Ralph," I replied

"We will be in touch with your agents to arrange a screen test."

"For real?" I exclaimed. Apparently, two miracles could happen in one day.

In the end, I got the part! This was not only my big break, but also the beginning of the most wonderful education a young actress could ever hope to receive. I had the greatest teacher in Mr. Poitier. Any actor could hardly dream it possible getting an opportunity to learn from one of the greatest Hollywood had seen. Above it all however, was that he was extremely kind and he felt very much like an uncle to me.

Here is one lesson he taught that I will never forget. One day on set while filming was going on, I was lost in an especially interesting chapter of a book, *The People's Almanac*, after all I was in a classroom, and did not hear my name when they called me to take my place on my mark.

"Sheryl Lee Ralph," said a deep voice. I jumped!

Mr. Poitier was standing over me, and everybody was watching. "What are you doing? He asked, looking at me very seriously.

"Reading a book," I said.

"Well, I'm just directing a movie here. So, why don't you just share with us what's got you so engrossed that you have no idea what is happening on the set."

"I can't."

Oh, he was not having it. "Yes, you can," he responded sternly.

Everyone was watching me, from the production assistants to the key grips. I was so embarrassed that my voice shook as I whispered. *"Cunnilingus."* I was so deeply embarrassed. I couldn't believe this was happening. Apparently, my voice wasn't low enough as I could hear muffled laughter all around me. Mr. Poitier didn't flinch. He paid no attention to the chuckling or whispers. Instead, he leaned down and looked at me— right in the eyes. "When you're on my set," he said quietly, "pay attention. I'm the director. I'm the one you should be reading. Understand? Good," he said. "Then get on your mark."

As horrified as I was by that whole situation, I will be forever grateful for the way he handled the situation and treated me. In that moment, he did not laugh along with everyone else. Instead, he used that moment to teach me something. Teachable moments are important, and I took his advice at heart. Anything I needed to learn about filmmaking, I could learn right there.

A DIVA knows there are lessons to be learned everywhere. This was a true education in the entertainment industry. I was going to be a star pupil. I had made a mistake, and I would learn from it. I watched everything and took it all in. I learned about production, costuming, and lighting. To this day, I know if my lighting is good or not, and I am not afraid to speak my mind if changes are needed. A DIVA knows to take an active part in her own life. She does not let anyone else take control. She takes part in and helps to form her own outcome. A real DIVA has a balanced enough ego to learn from her mistakes. To this day, being on my mark and ready to roll means something to me.

The film, *A Piece of the Action*, is a crime comedy about two thieves played by Bill Cosby and Sidney Poitier. They are blackmailed by James Earl Jones into going straight and working at a center for juvenile delinquents—really bad "juvies." Desperate to avoid prison time, they take the opportunity.

I played Barbara Hanley, one of the "juvies." Remember, this was 1977, and Black America was using the voice it had found in the '60s. It was exploding with years of pent-up anger. My character brought that anger, especially the young component, to the screen. In a four-minute monologue, I lashed out against the world by lashing out against those nearest me: The teachers who were trying to help me.

I will never forget filming that scene. There I am, nineteen-years-old and in my first film, playing my very first role with an Academy Award winner as my director. And what a role it was! Barbara was not at all like me. She was a rough, unhappy girl born into poverty. She would just as soon cuss you out for no reason than speak to you. I was going to get to know her and give her life.

"Time out. Time out, dammit," my monologue began. And from that moment, it was on! I just became someone else.

"If we all get jobs, it will blow your game," I said, my voice seething with anger. "Yeah, yo game, all you middle class, boogie-ass niggers. Don't blow smoke up my ass about no freaking job for us poor, deprived ghetto children. Now, if it wasn't for niggers like us, you all wouldn't make shit. And where do you all live? Not around here, I bet you that. My mama didn't raise no fool."

"What's happening is I can recognize a poverty pimp when I see one. What's happening is bourgeois bullshit." At one point, I even turned to Mr. Durrell, played by Mr. Poitier, and spit, "What do you all nig-gers make for this jive ass number you're running down on us, huh? $15, $20,000?"

Saying words like bullsh++, the F-word and the N-word were very disturbing to me. I didn't curse and it was difficult but that's what the role called for and I had to deliver. I am often asked how I created that character. Where a nice little girl like me could have found that kind of anger. After seeing the film, even my father was shocked.

"I know you're an actress, because I don't know who that girl is," he told me.

As an actress, that was a great compliment. I was, indeed, very different from the character, Barbara Hanley, yet, even as a young actress, I could under-stand her. She was a hard-edged child of poverty with a chip on her shoulder. I could understand her pain and ambition. I could feel her fire for life, bub-bling up inside of me. And I let her voice explode across the screen. Even today, Barbara is still relevant. And though a lot has changed, many young African American men and women are still fighting their way out of poverty. Burning to learn more and live better. Yearning to be understood and appreciated as human beings. We saw it in the protests after George Floyd's death: "Black Lives Matter!" If you can't say it, then they don't matter.

How did I disappear inside of that character? I knew that girl on a different level. As a child of integration, I always lived straddling the Black and White worlds.

My parents wanted the best for me. So, in the fourth grade, they had me take a test for a new school—an exclusive, private school. I had never seen anything like it before. Public schools had huge, concrete playgrounds—boys on one side, girls on the other, with the common area in-between. However, my new school was all green and there were no boy students at all. I knew I was somewhere special and had this feeling that I must be someone special to be allowed inside of those gates. What I did not realize was that many of my classmates and teachers wouldn't feel the same way about me. Being special wasn't a good thing, neither was being Black in that school.

That first morning, I had been so excited to put on my new school uniform. There were no uniforms in public school, and this was nothing like the uniform I wore for Girl Scouts. We had crisp white shirts, blue blazers, knee-length plaid skirts, knee-high socks, and brown wingtip shoes. Did I mention the tie? Yes, we had that, too. I loved it. I loved the whole ensemble, except the shoes.

As soon as I entered that huge front gate, I realized the uniform was not enough to make me fit in. No one else looked like me. No one else had the same kind of kink in her curls or full lips like mine. I looked at all of the girls dressed up and ready to learn on that first day. I thought, *"Who would be my new BFF and E—my new Best Friend Forever and Ever? Who will I do homework with and tell my secrets to?"* As I looked around something became immediately obvious. I was the only little Black girl in a sea of White people. The nuns who ran the school stood before us. Not one of them shared my color either.

The school was very organized. We lined up outside in the yard, walking quickly and quietly in single file to our classroom. I will never forget that first day. I took my assigned seat. I even remember where it was—the fourth one in the last row next to the windows. I looked outside. I started to cry. I was an outsider.

In my new school life, from 8:30 AM to 3:30 PM, the only Colored person, Black person, or Negro, I saw was in the Girls' Room mirror. Hmmm! Making friends was not easy, but I did it. These were the kinds of friends who found me entertaining. They wanted to feel my hair and understand why it could stand up on its own. They wanted to touch my skin, as though it would be different from theirs. I quickly discovered that it actually was. My skin was tougher. Through my indefatigable ancestors, it had learned years before how to toughen up.

When those girls called me names, I wouldn't let it hurt me. I let it just roll off my back into the abyss of America's mortal sin. I tried to believe what my mother always told me: "Sticks and stones will break my bones, but words will never hurt me." But those words did hurt. They used to say I had liver lips. Hmmm! Funny! I see so many of them now paying big money now to have lips like mine. They said I was ugly and weird. They used other words they probably heard from adults, saying things they probably didn't even understand themselves. I did not understand it either and I wasn't going to lose any sleep over it. I was learning something: how to keep moving forward and carry on. I was a little girl, but I had to stand strong. I had no other choice.

Then there were the other girls. The things they said were worse. "Hate" is a strong word, but I hated and still hate the "N" word. I tried back then to stand up for myself and waited, hopefully, for someone to stand up for me. Sometimes a lone voice in the crowd would tell the bullies to leave me alone. It is amazing what one voice can do. There is power in one. I just wish I had heard it more often.

Every Wednesday, some students would go downstairs to the small Music Room for our half-hour piano lesson. My dad was a master pianist and organist. With him being the orchestra conductor, I was expected to play piano as well. My piano teacher was a rigid young nun, with icy green eyes and red hair that peeked out of her veil. That woman made me uncomfortable. My fingers never seemed to hit the right notes when she was watching. And it didn't help that I had not practiced enough. One day, I left my classroom and went straight to my piano lesson. Sister was in a foul mood. My fingers stumbled over the keys, and I started over. I guess I started over one too many times, because she walked up behind me and slammed that piano lid shut, with a thud, just missing my fingers!

"You know," she said, "I don't have to take students like you." And she just looked at me with that cold, green gaze, then she sent me back upstairs to class. Running up those stairs, I was happy to get away from her.

When I opened the door to my classroom, I saw that my entire class was gone. I was confused. *Where are they? Why did they leave me?* I headed straight over to the principal's office, and they sent me in to see Mother Superior.

I told Mother Superior what had happened. I explained that my class was gone. I didn't know what to do. She acted as if I had done something wrong. She told me there were consequences for lying. She said sternly, "Liars are not tolerated at this school." She walked me back over to my classroom. I tried to keep up with her long, determined strides, watching her black habit billowing in the wind, almost hitting me in my face. *Why would Mother Superior think that I'm a liar?* When Mother Superior opened the door to the classroom, it was empty. I had been left behind. I was the only Black child in the school and somehow I had been forgotten. I mean, how could they just leave me behind? Until this day, I wonder why and how that happened.

Mother Superior looked down at me. "Go home," she said.

Why were these nuns so unkind? What had I done to make the piano teacher so angry? Why did my teacher and class leave me? Why did Mother Superior send me home in the middle of the day without even calling my parents? I just couldn't figure it all out. *Maybe they're right,* I thought.

Maybe I did something wrong. Maybe I didn't practice enough. Maybe I was a bad girl. Hmmm. These were the minions of Christ...humm.

At the end of fourth grade, my father was offered the job of Assistant Principal at a Long Island High School and I was so happy to be leaving my current school. In pursuit of the best for their children, my parents tried to enroll me in yet another private school when we moved to New York. *I* made it plain, in no uncertain terms, that was not happening. I told them I was going to public school. They must have heard something convincing in my voice because they did not argue. A DIVA must be captain of her own ship.

Everything was better after that. I made lots of friends in my new public school. Now, these were the kind of friends who kept in touch with me and some even found me years later, on Facebook. By middle school, I had found a place for myself in the school hierarchy. I ran for class office, competed in sports, sang in the choir, played in the orchestra and school plays. I was busy! I fit in, sort of. Even so, what happened in the fourth grade has never left me. Those experiences are still there, and they still hurt. I have learned to push them far away deep inside and I carry on.

Sometimes a DIVA has to leave the hurt behind. To carry it with you, only makes it hurt worse. Everyone to some degree has felt like an outsider. We have all had our own version of that piano teacher telling us that we are not good enough, smart enough, or even the right color or gender. It never feels good. I have learned that when people start telling you how unworthy you are, what they are really saying is how deeply unworthy they feel about themselves.

As for Barbara Hanley, I could play that character, because I knew her pain. I understood how she felt having her teacher call her dumb. I learned as an actress to call upon my personal memories as inspiration. I had to bring that hurt little girl to the surface, look her straight in the eyes without flinching and say, "Girl, we are in this together." I embraced Barbara and I love her still. On the set, I felt comfortable and safe enough to let her and all of her hurt and anger live out loud.

Years later, I now know the truth. Nothing I could have done would have made a difference. Nothing would have made those nuns like me because they did not like themselves. Nothing would have changed the deep knee jerk reaction of racism even in the face of the church. With Mr. Poitier's lessons learned, I found myself moving forward.

We've all heard it. Yes? Many men in Hollywood use their power to seduce young girls. That was not Mr. Poitier's style. He was a man of decency with daughters of his own. Getting that part was one of the greatest gifts I had ever been given. Sidney Poitier as a director had the utmost respect for his cast and me, further setting the tone of what respectability looks like for one of the best Hollywood men, and what I would come to look for on future projects. Unfortunately, that was not always the case.

As for co-starring with Bill Cosby, well, he was an absolute, nonstop ball of energy. He was a wild man with his big ol' afro and '70s suits. When he came to the set, the vibe changed immediately. The mood lightened as he made people laugh, similar to what it was like having Jamie Foxx or Bernie Mac on the set of *Moesha* years later. I did not spend much time with Mr. Cosby on the set of *A Piece of the Action*. Most of my scenes were shot in the classroom. The movie itself was a classroom to me, and not all of the lessons were easy to learn.

The last time I saw Mr. Cosby was in Philadelphia, where my husband, Vincent Hughes, is a State Senator. Yes, I got deliciously married. It was a beautiful Veteran's Day event and Vincent had organized a very large program to celebrate the move of the hidden All Wars Memorial to Colored Soldiers and Sailors statue to a prominent site in Logan Square, along the Benjamin Franklin Parkway. A U.S. Veteran himself, and a Philly native, Mr. Cosby was the guest speaker. It was obvious he was having serious trouble with his eyesight. I was seated right next to him. He couldn't see me, but he recognized my voice.

"Sheryl Lee Ralph," he said with a big smile. "When they call my name, please, walk me to the podium." I did.

He gave a heart-felt speech to an audience who cheered him. The next day, nothing would be the same for Mr. Cosby.

Young and fresh off *A Piece of the Action*, I did not know then that the world was far more complicated for Black actresses beyond Mr. Poitier's safe haven. In Hollywood, it was not enough to be talented. I was choosing to walk on a road that still needed to be built. It was a time when, as I later told *The New York Times*, Black actresses had limited options in terms of casting; or as I put it, we play an extraordinary range of welfare mamas and hookers, naked or dead.

Even if I had known the odds, I would not have let it stop me. Like any good DIVA, I would never let anybody tell me what I was or was not capable of doing. That said, nothing was going to come easy. But good DIVAs never back down from their dreams, because they know their dreams are worth fighting for. And fight I would. And like in fourth grade, I'd find my tribe elsewhere, even if it took forever.

▼

DIVA Lesson Three
Learn to Leave the Hurt Behind.
Carrying It with You Only Makes It Hurt More.

CHAPTER FOUR

OUT ON A LIMB

Robert De Niro gave me a reality check that I will never forget. We were on the set of the movie *Mistress*, where I played his strong-willed girlfriend—okay, side chick…mistress The scene was in a car, and we were chatting in-between takes as the production crew did some lighting adjustments.

Robert turned to me, "Sheryl Lee," he said in that real New York accent of his, "You are really talented. No, I mean you're really talented. But do you want to know the truth about this business? You're going to have to climb that mountain and wave the red flag. Let them know that you're here because Hollywood is not looking for the Black girl."

Wow! He just said that: "Hollywood is not looking for the Black girl." A true reality check because this was 1992. If he thought Hollywood was tough on the Black girl in the '90s, he should have tried starting out being a Black girl in Hollywood when I did.

He was right about it being hard, but here was where he was wrong. Hollywood was always looking for the Black girl. I mean, who else was going to play the prostitute? And I am not talking about the prostitute with the heart of gold either. You know that prostitute because you have seen her a million times. She sells her body because she has no other choice. She has to feed her baby, make her rent, cover her tuition, but she is a good person underneath it all. She is Julia Roberts in *Pretty Woman*. She is Shirley MacLaine in *Sweet Charity*. She is Nicole Kidman in *Moulin Rouge*.

Every actress knows that a hooker with a heart of gold is the kind of role that can make you a star. Just ask Julia Roberts. Still, it is not the same for a Black actress, not that I do not love a challenging part, because I do. But the Black prostitute is a whole different thing—at least that is how I saw it in the late '70s. The Black prostitute always got killed first and always had a drug problem. No one ever had anything nice to say about her. Then she's shot and left for dead. And the vast majority of the time, she would be left dead and naked.

When I decided to become an actress, these weren't the parts I would imagine myself playing. I wanted to play parts, such as, Diahann Carroll in the television show, *Julia*. Julia was a widow, raising her son, and doing the best she could to be a responsible woman and mother. She was beautiful, smart, and Black. Well, I loved that. It didn't take much time in Hollywood for me to understand the truth. It was an anomaly.

That show was called groundbreaking for a reason. There were rarely parts like that, that were good or realistic for a Black woman. I had dreams of waking up as beautiful as Judy Pace in *Brian's Song*. I wanted to make my mark in movies being beautifully Black or being the first Black woman to go where no man has gone before. I wanted to be like Lieutenant Nyota Uhura played by Nichelle Nichols in Star *Trek*.

Coming off of *A Piece of the Action*, I was ready for my life in show business to begin. The reviews of my performance were wonderful. And some people said I should be nominated for something. But I could not think about that. There was no time. I was too busy wondering, *Where was my next movie role?* I was young, eager, and God knows, I was willing to work hard. I wanted juicy, emotional parts that would challenge me as an actress. I wanted love scenes and death scenes and dialogues full of heartbreak and joy. And therein lies the rub…walking the tightrope of talent and racism was no joke.

I went on many auditions to play the Black prostitute or the welfare mama or the poor Black lady on the couch. I just couldn't do it. I just could not play those roles. Once in a while, a young actress would ask me how I had the guts to make those choices by saying no to any part. Well in my book no was a full sentence, but those decisions, every no, led to a ten-year wait until my next film role. Parts are hard to find, they tell me. I want to work, they always say. And I understand completely their longing to be working actresses. I wish I could tell you the exact reason I was so choosy about my roles, but it is not something I can easily explain. I just knew that I had other people to answer to. I never wanted to embarrass my family. Their pride in me was more important than any role or working as an actress at all. Most of all I wanted no regrets.

Years later I would jump at the chance to play the first Black transgender character on television on the Showtime series, *Barbershop* developed for TV by screenwriter John Ridley. As an actress, I embrace the opportunity to stretch myself with a role that was both groundbreaking and edgy, a trans woman in love? Once again, the character, Claire, was very different from me, and the role was well written. I was playing a human being with emotional depth, wants, real pain, and real dreams. I was also challenging myself as an actress. I may be a woman, but I could and did play the part of that man turned trans woman, and I loved her.

Now, would I take that role today? Probably not when there are so many talented trans-actors in the industry now like MJ Rodriguez, Angelica Ross, Laverne Cox, Flame Monroe, to name a few. Still, the actress in me sure would think about it, though it would be a risk. The risky roles I did not want and would not play are the pimp, the hoe, the druggie, and the woe-is-me.

Maybe I could not put it into words at that time, but I knew in my heart that I wanted more for myself as an actress and a young woman. I knew being portrayed in that way over and over and over again was detrimental to both the audience and my own well-being. Even today, I cringe at seeing certain Black images on Reality TV. Today though, there is also a new balance and I applaud it. The new balance of multifaceted, positive Black female role models and actresses gracing our TV screens. I'm happy to see Viola Davis, Kerry Washington, Regina King, Octavia Spencer, Issa Rae, Robin Thede, the cast of *Pose*, Zendaya, the brilliance that is Quinta Brunson and so many more changing perceptions and lighting up the screen. It feels good to be seen and not ignored.

You see, there has to be balance. My grandmother taught me an old saying. For her, it was more than just something to be said. It was something I was meant to live by, "When you walk into the room, the whole race enters with you." I took that to heart.

Looking back, I think I had a lot of guts. I wanted to work more than anything, but I would not betray my values. My worst fear was that I would be forced to call my Daddy and beg for money to buy a plane ticket home. Despite that fear, over and over I continued to refuse to play those kinds of roles. Now, I don't judge the women who took those parts. Some of them are still working, and they are good actresses—many of them beautiful and talented. Through my ten year film drought my peers would ask me over and over, why was I being so stubborn? I would just tell them the truth. Those parts are just not for me. Those parts are not who I am. I was still discovering who I was, and I was still finding my way in the world. If I ever even, just for a moment, considered the possibility of playing a hooker dead or alive, I would just think about my mom and dad sitting proudly in front of the TV, to watch my television debut as a dead, Black, naked whore. I could not do it. I did not ever want to play a part that my parents would not be proud of seeing me in. I wanted my grandmother and the folks at church to be proud of me, too. Worse than failing as an actress was the overwhelming fear that I had disgraced my family. Their approval meant the world to me, not to mention, my grandmother's saying stayed with me. I would not do anything I felt would disgrace my race either. Most of all I would never do anything to disgrace myself.

I blame and thank my parents for this stubbornness. They kept me grounded enough to say what I would and would not do. At that time, it was mostly what I would not do. And it was not easy—all of those disappointments. Getting called in to read for a big casting director, then handed a script page full of caricatured, 'ghettofied' dialogue that was written by some old white guy, who would never dream of going within ten miles of a real Black ghetto. And this old white guy was going to tell me how to be Black? How to sound Black? Sounds preposterous, doesn't it? Well, welcome to Hollywood baby.

But the world was changing. Black people and Black artists were finding their voices. There was anger and outrage. There was a cry for equality and change. Unfortunately, television isn't the real world.

And it was changing at a much slower pace. Casting agents were confused about what to do with someone like me. Upon my return to Hollywood after my Broadway stint in *Dreamgirls*, a big studio casting director told me, and his words still haunt me to this day. "Everybody knows that you're obviously a talented, beautiful, Black girl, but what do I do with a beautiful, talented Black girl? Put you in a movie opposite Tom Cruise? Do you kiss? Who goes to see that movie?"

His words were meant to harm me, but they only made me stronger. Even now, believe it or not, some find an interracial kiss on screen unnerving. Back then, the idea was practically laughable. No network would dare put that out there for America to see. At the very least there would be a huge outcry. Audience and advertisers alike. There would be protests too! And over a kiss. Imagine that. So, yes, my options were limited back then. Only a handful of Black television shows were around and those few walked a fine line between reality and pure stereotype. Those shows that Hollywood created back then to show their version of the true, authentic Black American experience—well, they were overwhelmingly created, produced, written, and directed by White people. The Black people had to be satisfied playing the Black people, White people conceived.

Redd Foxx actually walked away from his starring role on the hit show, *Sanford and Son*, because of a complete lack of Black directors and writers. It was his belief that the White producers and the publicity staff not only did not know about Black culture, but they also did not care to find out. And Mr. Foxx, might just have been right.

There is one audition I will never forget. I was up for a role in *Sanford Arms*, one of the three spin-offs of *Sanford and Son*. I got to read for a real big wig TV producer in Hollywood—Bud Yorkin. He was one of the show's creators and the kind of guy who could snap his fingers and make a struggling young actress into a star. I was excited and nervous. This was my big chance. This was one of the few network TV pilots with a Black cast and a young, female lead. And I had been called in to read for that plum role, and she was not a prostitute. After a lack of quality roles for young, Black women, this was the opportunity I had been praying for, waiting for, living for.

I got lots of sleep the night before. The next morning, I ate a healthy breakfast, took extra care in picking out my outfit, and doing my vocal warmups. When I got into that room with Mr. Yorkin, my nervousness just faded away. Just as in that moment with Mr. Poitier, I knew I had three minutes, and I was going to give it my best shot.

Mr. Yorkin, sitting with his assistant, nodded to me. I took a deep breath. Then I read my lines. I read my little heart out. I finished, flushed with happiness. I did a good job, and I knew it. I looked at Mr. Yorkin. I could only imagine my young face glowing and hopeful, just waiting for that tiny, little word that would change everything. The "yes" that would launch my career after so many nos.

Well, I got the part. Yes, I did!

I started the next week. After the table read I was on cloud nine. We wrapped the day, and I left the studio happy. And then I got that call from my agent and friend to this day, telling me that I had been fired. I immediately hung up the phone and called Mr. Yorkin's office.

"Here's the thing," he said. "You're just not right for the part. To be completely honest with you, well, you are just not Black enough."

I felt my whole body go numb. Did he just tell me I wasn't Black enough? He kept talking, probably telling me exactly how Black enough he believed I wasn't. I don't remember a word he said. I just remember looking at my obviously Black hands and they were shaking. I don't remember if I said goodbye. I don't remember anything. It was all just a blur.

I had been Black enough to be called in for numerous parts to play the Black prostitute, but I wasn't Black enough to play a Black with education and drive. What did that even mean? My ancestors had been African, and I wasn't Black enough? This wasn't like telling an actress she needed to lose twenty pounds or dye her hair a different color or even get a nose job. This man was saying that who I am and the identity I was born with was just not his definition of blackness. I didn't even want to know what that was to a man who was a guardian of stardom.

For a moment, I considered quitting everything. I thought about going home to my parents and having them hold my hand and tell me everything would be fine. That I had done my best in the face of American racism. But then my mother would bring up Med School or where I could find a good doctor to marry, and I'd be right back where I started. One thing about me, my gift, and my burden, is that I am not a quitter. And sometimes the word "no" just makes you want it more. Somehow, deep inside, I knew it would be okay, and the tide would turn, and somebody would do right by me, and one day I will have a body of work of which I am proud. And something else I knew? That man would not know a Black person if one was standing right in front of him.

That was a hard-learned DIVA life lesson—a no today, can be a yes tomorrow. Just ask Vice President Kamala Harris. There would be many other calls of a similar nature with the same results. I soon came to understand that if I chose to stay in Hollywood, this kind of rejection was bound to happen again, again, and again. The noes for me would never change. So, what do you do, my lovely DIVAs in training when faced with this kind of maddening madness? Do you continue to take a risk on your dream? Do you let go of those dreams? Do you, as the visionary man Langston Hughes once wrote, let them dry up like a raisin in the sun? Well, I think we both know the answer to that: "H to the no!"

For here is the truth. Life is a risk. Life is a risk when the light turns red, and you cross the street thinking everyone is going to stop. What if someone doesn't? Life is a risk when you take out a credit card and buy something on the Internet. What if someone takes your name and steals your identity? Life is a risk when you get married and say the vows of lifetime commitment. Will that other person feel the exact same way until death do you part? The answer is this: I have no idea. The truth is life can be hard, and there are no set answers, but what is the alternative? Death is. And that is not much of an alternative.

Life is a risk, and life is for living. So go on and go after what you want. And when people tell you that you are crazy, or that it will never happen, or that you are not Black enough or White enough, that you're too fat, too thin, too young, too old, too smart, or just not dumb enough, well, who says they know everything or anything at all? They are just people like you and me, facing their fears and trying to live their dream even if backwards. You can never be sure. You might just see them years later and they might just look at you with their eyes full of new understanding, and say they made a mistake. Or, as Mr. Bud Yorkin put it…oh yeah, that Bud Yorkin, when I ran into him at a Hollywood function decades later: "Not casting you in that show was one of my greatest mistakes. And I'm sorry. Sheryl Lee Ralph, you are a wonderful actress."

I smiled and said, "Thank you!"

I could see it in his eyes. He knew the pain he had caused me, and there was no point in holding a grudge. Besides, I am a firm believer in letting bygones be, well...gone; except of course, when you're writing a book for your fellow DIVAs and want to make a point. Anyway, I am sure we were both thinking the same thing. How that little show—the one I had not been Black enough for—was so awful that NBC pulled it from the airways after only four episodes. And that is how the cookie crumbles.

▼

DIVA Lesson Four
Life is a risk.
So, take that risk and live your life!

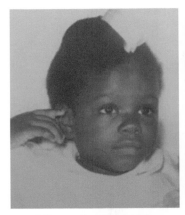

Me, at 2 years old.   Me, as a young actress.

My Dad, Dr. Stanley Ralph.

My Mom, Ivy Ralph.

Dad & Me.
I was 23 years old.

My Grandmother,
Julia Ralph.

Me and my children, Coco, and Etienne, at DIVAS Simply Singing.

My Family visiting the Muhammad Ali Museum when I was inducted.

Coco and Me wearing tees promoting human rights at WalkGoodLA, founded by my son, Etienne.

Me, daughter Coco, Harry Belafonte & son, Etienne.

My Husband, the Honorable Senator Vincent Hughes.

My daughter, Coco, Me, and my mom, Ivy Ralph.

**My very first film role in *A Piece of the Action*
with Sidney Poitier.**

Broadway 1981, *Dreamgirls*, Jennifer Holliday, Me, and Loretta Devine.

Jennifer Holliday and Me.   **Me and Loretta Devine.**

The Distinguished Gentlemen, Me, Eddie Murphy,
and other cast members.

Mistress, Me with Robert De Niro.

Mighty Quinn, Me with Denzel Washington.

Me in the
Flintstones.

Jon Voight and Me, *Ray Donovan.*

Me and Whoopi Goldberg.

DIVAS Simply Singing.

Miss J, Jennifer Hudson, and Me.

Me and
Lauryn Hill.

Me and
Jennifer
Lewis.

On the set of *Instant Mom*.

Me and Brandy.

**Me as Madame Morrible in the Broadway Show *Wicked*.
Relaxing before going on stage.**

Me at the Warner Brothers Studios with *Abbott Elementary* banner draping the wall.

Me with *Abbott Elementary* show creator, Quinta Brunson.

**My Family celebrating before the
Emmy Award Ceremony.**

Emmy, Me, and my Husband Senator Vincent Hughes at 2022 Emmy Awards.

Me and Michael Keaton at the Emmy Awards 2022.

On the set of *Abbott Elementary*, Flowers from Oprah Winfrey. It took four men and a truck to deliver.

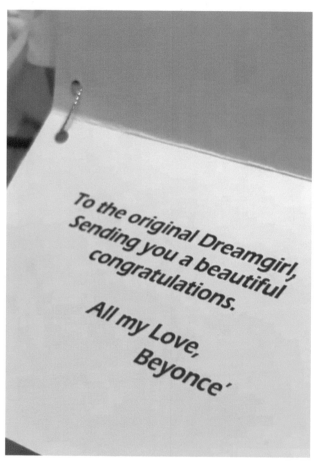

I received flowers & this card from Beyoncé Knowles.

Receiving the Order of Jamaica OJ award from the Most Honourable Sir Patrick Allen, Governor General of Jamaica. Yes, I am now "The Honourable!"

My Warrior Woman Heritage Collage.

Just Me.

CHAPTER FIVE

A DIVA DOESN'T QUIT

I did not leave Hollywood. If anything, that *Sanford* experience made me push ahead even harder. Yes, Mr. De Niro, I waved that red flag, and I kept waving. In fact, I am still waving it. I went back to pounding the pavement, but now with a renewed energy.

Show biz is full of rejection. You will get a hundred noes to that one important yes. Understanding that reality I grew stronger and more confident, and those noes seemed less and less important. I just had to keep working on my craft and keep my look and outlook fresh. Faith kept me going knowing that I was born to perform, and no other life path would make me as happy. Holding on to my faith put everything, even rejection, in perspective. Remember, DIVA in training: people who have made it to great heights, struck out on their own, and took chances—it wasn't always easy for them. And it will not always be easy for you, but it will be worth the climb. Don't give up on you.

I did not know it then, but I was already waving that red flag. I stuck it out taking classes, praying like my mother had taught me, and by keeping the faith. Then one day, the tide turned. I got another part. The part was not huge, under five lines, but I was blown away. I would be playing George Jefferson's secretary on the hit TV sitcom, *The Jeffersons*. In an odd way, it seemed fated.

Sherman Hemsley, who played George Jefferson on *The Jeffersons* was someone I had looked up to for years. In high school, I had a chance to meet him when he was in the Broadway musical, *Purlie*. I loved that musical. Sherman and his co-star, Melba Moore, were amazing and I clearly remember sitting in the audience and being mesmerized. I could see myself up on stage one day.

I had gotten the chance to meet Sherman briefly backstage, and he was very nice to me. I was just a high school kid, and his warmth had a huge effect on me. So, all these years later, when I had my first real part on a TV show in which he was starring, it felt good. George Jefferson was an over-the-top character, while Sherman Hemsley always seemed a bit shy and unassuming. On *The Jeffersons* set, I told him how much he inspired me. He seemed to know how important this first, real TV job was to me, because he went out of his way to be kind and supportive. Those early kindnesses from genuinely beautiful people never leave you and seeds you with a sensitivity that makes paying it forward or backwards rewarding.

More than a decade after I met him on *The Jeffersons*, I was recurring on *Designing Women* as Etienne Tousaint Bouvier, Anthony Las Vegas's fiancé. When they needed someone to play my father for our wedding episode, I suggested that Sherman be cast. The producers agreed, and it was extraordinary to have Sherman Hemsley on the set with me. We had not seen each other in years, and we had a lot of catching up to do. I reminded him how he encouraged me as a high school student when I saw him on Broadway. I thanked him for treating me like an equal on *The Jeffersons*, especially since he was number one on the call sheet. And let me tell you, series regulars can be notoriously nasty to the guest stars. I was just a young actress in her first, real TV role. It would have been just as easy for him to ignore me, but instead, he supported me. For all of that, I told him that I was forever grateful. Sherman told me he had followed my career and was especially thrilled that just like him, I had been on Broadway. He told me how proud it made him to see that I had grown into a strong young woman with a thriving career of my own. We couldn't and wouldn't stop smiling. In our last scene together on *Designing Women*, all of those years of struggle and triumph were right there with us, playing out in that scene. We both had fought for our careers, and here we were, both going strong. We stood there on the set of that hit show and Sherman looked at me as he said his final line to me.

"I just love you so much."

Instantly, we both burst into tears. The whole audience erupted with a spontaneous "Ahhhhhh." That moment did not require acting from either one of us. We shared a legacy.

The Jeffersons role led to more auditions, which led to a guest starring role that led to another. And before I knew it, that 19 year-old-girl who told her dad, "Right now I have to be here," from a telephone booth at the Los Angeles airport...well, that girl was a little older, a little wiser, and she had an actual, undeniable television acting career. And she did it without playing any parts that would have embarrassed her family or, more importantly, herself.

Success can and does happen, and it can happen without compromising yourself. It might be harder to get there, but in the end, you will be able to live with the decisions you made. And here are the keys: Never give up and know just how far you will go to make it or get that job. Yes, DIVAs know their bottom line. If you are faced with a decision you're unsure about, or feel might compromise you, imagine some people important to you, and picture their faces. How will they feel if they see you do this or that? I have never played a part that would embarrass my family. And I have never slept with someone to get a part. That is a recipe for disaster. If you sleep with someone for a part, you know what you will get? Screwed, royally in every sense of the word.

To be clear, I never would let any decision I made even get me near the casting couch. Of course, I had a

95

few inescapable moments. There was the famous promoter who, after seeing me in *Dreamgirls*, took me to a very expensive lunch to discuss my future in entertainment. I soon realized, with his hand creeping up my thigh, that he was interested in a completely different kind of entertainment. A DIVA gracefully walks away. Then there was the young producer, who actually had the power to make things happen for me if I just slept with him on that trip to Vegas and did a little something-something. I knew my bottom line. I knew how far I would go, and it was not to his casting couch. And I would simply say this: "I don't do that. But if you cast me first, then maybe I'll sleep with you, but that would be only if I want to." I never wanted to.

What it comes down to is this: I am not a gambling woman—not with my career, not with my money, and certainly not with my body. I know that sleeping with someone with the hope of that person casting you is a bad bet. And I don't like to lose money, let alone myself.

A DIVA lesson: Giving up your cookies won't get you anything but well, eaten alive. It was a rough climb back then. Today, I thank God for Tarana Burke founding #MeToo and for Christy Haubegger's Times Up. Women's empowerment movements elevating Hollywood and global consciousness around obstacles women encounter daily is way past due.

Eventually, my talent, training, and drive were a winning combination, and I could rely on them to carry me forward. Only a handful of shows had all-Black casts, and somehow, I found my way on enough of them to make a difference in my life and my career. True, these shows were not perfect in their depiction of real Black people, however, they gave an African American audience a chance to see characters of their own color, with actual believable storylines. In that way, they were ahead of their time. And I am proud to have been a part of them.

To this day, people still come up to me, or hit me up on social media, because they remember seeing me in *Good Times*, when I played JJ's "bougie" girlfriend who couldn't possibly go bowling because, "The night air is murder on my lip gloss." Lord! Hmmm!

They remember my being on *The Jeffersons* and want to know what went on behind the scenes. The truth about those shows, the forerunners and Black sitcoms that paved the way for shows like *The Cosby Show, Moesha*, and *Blackish*, is that there were so few shows and opportunities for Black actors; we felt lucky to be working at all. Now, this was before there were entire lineups of shows, let alone networks featuring Black folks.

When people ask about those early shows, I know they want the juicy gossip on catfights and the chaos. Well, I don't have those stories to tell, at least not from that time in my career. Of course, things are always changing. And future television sets would offer more drama, but more about *Moesha* at another time.

When I first started out in the business, I felt a sense of community. I will never forget my time on *The*

Jeffersons. That was a show the likes of which America had never seen before. And if you think about it today, it doesn't sound that edgy: A Black couple who become successful and move on up to the wealthier lifestyle with a "dee-luxe" condo on the East Side. And that lyric from their famous theme song, "Movin' on Up": "Fish don't fry in the kitchen," pure gold. More controversial than the Black people living the upper-class lifestyle on the East Side was the interracial couple who lived downstairs from the Jeffersons. Pretty tame stuff by today's standards, but in the late '70s, Norman Lear was pushing the envelope hard, and some people found the show absolutely shocking.

Perhaps the actors were not always aware that what they were doing was so ahead of the time. But they knew they were doing something special and watched out for each other. Roxie Roker, who played Helen Willis, was the Black part of the interracial couple on *The Jeffersons*. She must have understood the interracial prejudice well because in real life, her husband was White. That was pretty brave for that time, and even to some extent to this day. Interracial marriage only became legal in America in 1967 and still there are states that don't recognize them.

Roxie was an elegant woman, with a kind heart. I was just starting out, and she was generous and helpful. She was simply wonderful at giving me advice in her dressing room, and even invited me over to her home for Thanksgiving, because she knew I would be lonely with my family all the way across country. Her husband, Sy, was a nice man. And, Lord, he loved him some Roxie. And I will never forget their son—a bright forward-thinking teenager, with his modern-cut 'fro and argyle vest, always hanging around the set, and taking everything in. Roxie was so proud of him. "My son, Lenny," she would tell me, "He's going to be a great artist. Just you wait."

In the end, little Lenny Kravitz did just fine for himself. Whenever I see him—a grown man with a beautiful child of his own, Zoe—all those memories flood back. I remember him on the set saying, always with respect and always with manners, "Ms. Ralph, when are you going to let me write a song for you?" Maybe someday he will.

Roxie passed away of breast cancer. She was still young and still very vibrant. She touched my life in a special way, and I will never forget her glowing spirit. She grew ill and lost her hair, but she never lost her warmth or dignity, not even for a second. She kept her door open to others as long as she could. Her death was a great loss.

Things picked up quickly after I got that first part on *The Jeffersons*. The '80s had just begun and everything I had worked for was beginning to pay off. I had a real television career, and there were new opportunities every day. I was a working actress and determined to keep working. I fought hard for my career, and I was enjoying every moment of success, because I'd earned it.

Then just like that I got a call asking me to give up everything. Did I want to go to New York and audition for a musical? If I got the part, I would have to leave behind what I'd worked so hard for in Hollywood. Yes, theater was my first love, ever since that first audition for Dr. Bettenbender on the Douglas Campus of Rutgers University. I know that center stage is my home and where I felt most alive. Still, did I want to leave the glamor and the huge audience of television? Was I willing to take a big pay cut and work myself to the bone doing eight shows a week after having worked hard to establish my career in Hollywood?

If you know me at all, by now the answer is obvious. Of course, I would, and yes, I did!

▼

DIVA Lesson Five
A No Today Can Be Yes Tomorrow,
So Hold On To Your Dreams and Keep It Moving.

CHAPTER SIX

CHAOS IS A FRIEND OF MINE

Some musicals go down in history for their innovation and acclaim. Then there are the ones that go down in history for a completely different reason. They were notorious flops!

Reggae was in the second category. *Reggae* was to be producer Michael Butler's follow up to his smash, Broadway hit, *Hair*—nothing heavy-handed, just peace, love, reggae music, and ganja. There were some elaborate, colorful costumes, sexy rude boys in leather on motorbikes. There were Jamaican Rastafarians celebrating Judaism, complete with stunning choreography, happy, trippy, musical numbers. There was all that, but the big question, what was the musical about?

Well, the plot of all great musicals and movies is the same: Boy meets girl; boy loses girl; boy gets girl back again. In this musical, a girl named Faith, a famous Jamaican singer returns to the island to find herself. While there, she also finds her lost love, Esau, played by Philip Michael Thomas, of *Miami Vice* fame. You remember that TV series? Anyway, in *Reggae* he has become a ganja farmer/ low-key drug dealer.

With a production that included names like Michael Butler and Melvin Van Peebles as producers, *Reggae* also had Michael Kamen as Musical Director. Michael blessed me with a wonderful song, "Everything that Touches You." Oh, He was a lovely man and a great talent. Some stellar Jamaican artistes were on the production team as well—Harrison Stafford, Kendrew Lascelles, Ras Karbi, Max Romeo, and Jackie Mittoo; with that kind of talent, it should have been a hit. Well, you can't win them all. This was the kind of show Broadway had never seen before. And people wouldn't see it for long. *Reggae* opened on March 27, 1980, and closed April 13, for a total of 21 performances. The show closed almost as fast as it opened.

Of course, when I got the call to audition for *Reggae*, I did not know all of this. All I knew was this Broadway show was in previews, and was going to open in ten days, and they needed a star leading lady NOW! as the beauty queen cast to play Faith had just been fired. Word got around the showbiz world that she was hired for her looks and not for her acting abilities—a classic Broadway tale. Now that the show was about to open, there was one big problem, and it was obvious. She could not act to save her life or the show.

A friend of mine and friend to this day, Jeffrey Anderson-Gunter who was in the company, knew about the situation and called me. I had just been fired from director/producer Stewart Ostrow's musical,

Swing. Quick summary: a *Midsummer's Night's Dream* musical centered around a baseball game with four downtown White kids and four uptown Black kids. Fill it out with a jazzy score. Hit or flop? Flop! On the road to D.C, Ostrow fired all four of the Black actors in the cast, because as he put it, "we no longer fit stylistically in the show." He and the whole company left us in Delaware and went on to open at the Kennedy Center where they quickly closed. Bobby LuPone and Janet Eilber, who went on to become Artistic Director of the Martha Graham Dance Company, could not save that show. It had not been an easy production from day one, but I didn't understand why they just left us in Delaware. I know the show must and will go on, but I mean! Really? I cried until my nose ran and my eyes turned as red as rubies. I am talking the original ugly cry. Oh, I was devastated.

So, when Jeffrey called me, telling me to, "stop the crying and get on the first train smoking back to New York," I did what he told me. He knew Michael Butler would hire me if he saw me. The next morning, I was back in Manhattan, standing at the stage door of the Biltmore Theatre, with my suitcase in hand.

One door closes and a stage door opens.

I had always dreamed of being on Broadway. There is nothing like the excitement of performing for a live audience. In the case of the musical *Reggae,* it was all the way live! Once again, I had no idea what was in store, but it did not matter. This was Broadway and I was going to dive in headfirst as any true DIVA would.

Michael Butler, the hippie millionaire producer, was big time. He was the visionary who took a little off-Broadway hippie musical, with a crazy little script, and turned it into the hugely successful Broadway musical *Hair*.

Reggae, originally titled, *Irie*, was meant to be the successful follow up to *Hair* with the same unique hippie-inspired esthetic, with reggae music thrown in for flavor. There were hopes of a musical that would be revolutionary. When I arrived at the Biltmore Theatre stage door, the entire cast was milling around, praying that the show would go on. You could feel the tension in the air. After all, it was 10 days until the opening and there was no leading lady. After one preview, it was obvious that the beauty queen was not a Broadway baby.

My friend Jeffrey found me. His face lit up like that of a thirsty man who had seen a waterfall in the Sahara. He took me by the hand to meet Michael Butler. I introduced myself and Michael Butler opened the stage door and I walked on to that stage, and I was at home. Michael took a seat in the audience, his face a stone mask. He asked musical director Michael Kaman to teach me "Everything that Touches You." I began to sing, and Michael Butler didn't even let me finish. He handed me a script and had me read. I used the Jamaican accent I had learned from my mother. Michael Butler perked up and I was hired on the spot. Just like Dorothy, I had been lifted up into a tornado and landed in Oz. The days that followed would be an exciting blur.

I barely had time to call family and friends. Within hours of the audition, I was being given a crash course in Broadway, while trying to remember the lines, the songs, the choreography and blocking for a show that opened in ten days. There was no time for me to be nervous, let alone fully appreciate that I was opening as the lead, the star, in a Broadway show! Two days later, I was on stage for the critics' preview still holding a script in my hand. Imagine!!

The whole experience was exciting chaos. Working on stage with a cast is a team effort, and it requires a sense of trust. We had to trust that each other knew his or her lines, and that they would give you your cues. The lighting and sound people depended on you to move to the right place at the right time, so they would know their cues as well. The whole show should tick like a tightly wound watch. You know, the ones they used to wind up in order for them to run.

Reggae was chock-full of talent. Dancers—Kiki Shepard, Brenda Braxton, Ralph Gilmore and Obba Babatundé, a triple-threat performer who had just returned from touring with Liza Minnelli; singer Louise Robinson; Jamaican actors; and my close friends, Jeffrey Anderson-Gunter, and Tommy Pinnock as well as the great Calvin Lockhart who had starred in many Blaxploitation films. Ah! He was so beautiful— unfortunately, even with all of that talent, it was not enough to keep the show afloat. We opened the day of the transit strike and closed around the time of the garbage strike, twenty-one days later. It seemed the gray-haired, Broadway-matinee audiences—well, they didn't quite like or understand the concept of Black dreadlock, Rastafarian, Jamaican Jews, smoking ganja, and dancing with the Star of David to a Reggae beat across the Broadway stage. To tell you the truth, I didn't quite understand the show myself.

So, my Broadway career seemed as though it would end just as quickly as it started. Or so I thought. But the world is funny that way, my DIVA friends. Sometimes one stage door has to close for another to open really wide.

Tom Eyen, the genius playwright, was in the audience on one of those empty matinee days. Imagine a theater that holds at least 1,000 people with only 16 people in the audience. Oooo. That's enough to break an actor's heart and spirit. After the matinee, Tom Eyen came backstage.

Tom Eyen had written for Bette Midler, when she was entertaining in those infamous New York bathhouses. He was a smart, edgy writer and did not mind pushing the envelope of his work to the artistic edge. Maybe he could see the future of *Reggae* before the rest of us because he was more interested in telling me about a new project he was working on and suggested that I audition for it.

"Hmmm, I might have your next show", he told me. "It doesn't have a name yet, but it's a hit."

How could I know that because of that one, little backstage conversation, my life was about to change forever? I was only twenty-three years old. A month earlier, I had been fired from a big flop of a show. Now, here I was back in New York in another show (destined to flop), and this man says he might have my next part in a show without a name and it's going to be a hit. Go figure.

Everyday brought something new and unexpected. Yet, I was doing what I loved. And in that uncertainty was a great sense of excitement. When I look back at the young girl I was, giddy with energy and full of possibilities, woo, I wish I could take her hand. "Take a deep breath," I'd tell her. "Take a deep breath and get ready for the ride of your life."

Looking back, my DIVA sisters and brothers, over the next few years, would give me some of the highest and lowest moments in my life. There would be confusion and anger, elation, and undeniable joy. And now as I reflect on everything, well, this DIVA would not take a moment of it back.

That little show Tom Eyen was developing for Nell Carter wouldn't stay unnamed for long. After a long workshop process at the Public Theatre with Joseph Papp, who tagged it Project #9, it would go into an even longer workshop process with Michael Bennett, before it became *Dreamgirls*. And *Dreamgirls* would really be revolutionary—not to mention to all of us involved, a revelation.

▼

DIVA Lesson Six
Chaos Is the Natural Way of The World.
Work Through It.

CHAPTER SEVEN

MY TURN

When *Reggae* closed, I was disappointed, really disappointed. It was cold outside, then I was hit with the even colder reality that the show was over when that closing notice went up. I'd had a taste of Broadway and now I knew I wanted more. That said, even with the Broadway show under my belt, and a personal invitation to audition for Tom Eyen's new, unnamed, going-to-be-a-hit musical, I was a mess of nerves in the waiting room of the audition.

The room was packed with Black women of many shades and ages. All of whom could not just sing, but "sang!" Hmmm! You could see the anticipation on their faces as each one waited for her own three minutes in the room. Musicals with Black leads rarely grace Broadway. That might be why they called it "The Great White Way." There were some shows, like *The Wiz, Purlie, Eubie! Sophisticated Ladies, Timbuktu,* and *Bubbling Brown Sugar,* however, there never seemed to be enough opportunities, especially for young, Black actresses.

No one wanted to screw up this opportunity to play something other than the sexy siren; the wise mammy character with a short solo in the second act; or chorus girl number four: Black.

I found a place to sit. I waited. And it felt like hours before a man with a clipboard came out and called my name. The moment I entered the room and Tom Eyen smiled at me; my whole body relaxed. He sat behind a long table with a few other men who lacked his enthusiasm and looked either exhausted or bored.

"Sheryl Lee," he said, exhaling with great drama. "Are you ready to sing for us, darling?"

"Yes, I am. Thank you." Oh, those manners my mother had drilled into me were still there. Before I could open my mouth to sing my prepared audition song, he cut me off.

"Sing us something from church—the first thing that comes into your head."

My mind went blank. Being a quietly raised Episcopalian, Gospel was not my forte. I only visited the Baptist church once a month or so because my dad was the organist at Zion Baptist. So, I just opened up my mouth and sang the first thing that came into my head—a pure and simple "Ave Maria." When I finished, the room was silent. *Oh, I really messed this one up*, I thought to myself. *Why didn't I prepare better? But how could I know?* (Sigh.)

I saw one of the men behind the table roll his eyes. He leaned back with a sigh. I could tell they had had a long day.

"Thank you, Sheryl Lee," Tom said.

"You're welcome." I left the room.

I took my seat back in the waiting room (sigh), where we had been asked to stay until we were dismissed.

He asked for Gospel, I chastised myself. *And I gave him Ave Maria! I should just leave now and go home right now. I should just get on the plane and head right back to Hollywood. I had a nice run of it here in New York. I gave it my best shot. I only hope they haven't forgotten about me in California.* Nevertheless, I sat there and waited anyway. Of course, I did.

The day passed in a fog. Periodically, the man with the clipboard would call names.

"Thank you for coming," he would say. Women would hold back tears, or mutter angrily to themselves as they gathered their belongings. Some shot straight to the elevator in a huff. The day felt like eternity, as different combinations of girls were brought in, and others were asked to leave. It was like an early *American Idol*, except brutal.

They did not call me in to sing again. And I had no idea why they just kept me there hanging around.

Maybe it was a mistake, I thought. I waited for something to happen, and I waited.

Hours later, finally, something did happen.

"Loretta Devine, Ramona Brooks." I reached down to gather my bag. "And Sheryl Lee Ralph," said the man. "Could you come in? And the rest of you may leave. Thank you for your time."

And the rest of you can leave?

I had no idea at that moment how much my life was about to change. As he said those three words as familiar as my own heartbeat: Sheryl Lee Ralph, I never knew I was about to make a transition from struggling young actress, Sheryl Lee Ralph, to Sheryl Lee Ralph Broadway star! In the future, I would be called many names besides Sheryl Lee. I would be called DIVA, a role model, and a rebel. I had no idea; the next few years would bring the adoration of many and the fear of others. There would be admiration shown toward me that would make me blush and criticism so hard I would grit my teeth. To some, I would represent the breaking down of barriers and the opening of doors for other young actresses who looked like me. To others, no matter the success I would have, I would never go beyond being just a Black actress in a White industry. As one agent told me, "Don't be like that Diana Ross. Remember your place."

Don't be like that Diana Ross. Remember your place. Hmmm.

Well in that moment I knew, whatever place Miss Ross occupied, that's just the place I wanted to be. Of course, I had no idea of all of the things I would become, or all of the experiences yet to come. And I'm glad I didn't. The next stage of my life would be one of the roughest and most exciting journeys I could possibly imagine.

In so many ways, I was still a girl. I don't think one could ever be ready for the kind of events that would follow, no matter how young or old you were. The words rang in my head: *And Sheryl Lee Ralph.*

This was just the beginning.

▼

DIVA Lesson Seven
Don't Ever Believe Your Own Press.
Stay Humble and In a State of Gratitude.

CHAPTER EIGHT

NEW MOUNTAINS TO CLIMB

Few people believed in Project #9. To many, a show based around three young girls—three young Black girls—well, nothing like that had ever been done. This musical, as Tom Eyen saw it, would tell the story of a trio of young Black singers from Chicago, with big voices and even bigger dreams. In fact, they would be called "The Dreams." And the musical would follow their rise to international stardom.

Nothing was set in stone. In those early stages, the show was only a concept - and a concept strange enough to turn off the majority of mainstream Broadway backers. "What kind of an audience would Project #9 bring?" they would ask. This was not standard Broadway stuff. Unlike classic Americana musicals, such as, Oklahoma, there were no dancing cowboys or pretty blonde, milk-maid-looking White girls, singing about the dream man that would come and sweep them off of their feet.

Project #9 was not the kind of material thought to pull in a crowd. And although it was only said in private conversations, few believed a cast led by Black women would bring in a mainstream audience. Nothing like Project #9 had been done before: a cast of female characters, and strong Black female characters at that, was truly ahead of the times.

One of the few musicals of a somewhat ethnic cast to receive widespread fame, *West Side Story*, had cast a White woman to play Maria, the Puerto Rican lead. There was no camouflaging the Black faces that made up the future cast of Project #9, that is, if anyone believed in the show enough to give it a chance. Tom Eyen, true to the nature of a true dreamer, never gave up.

The first series of rehearsals for Project #9, known to some as a workshop, were financed by theater legend Joseph Papp. A workshop is where a musical is given creative space to grow and take shape. The cast is important to this process, and we were deeply connected to the making of the show, often helping to write and arrange songs or helping to write the show itself by improvising dialogue.

Tom Eyen had originally intended the project to be a star vehicle for Nell Carter, who had just won a Tony for her work in *Ain't Misbehavin.'* It's hard to imagine those early days now that Project #9 turned *Dreamgirls* has gone on to become legendary, at a time when there was just the circle of us sitting around the table. We spent the rehearsals practicing early variations of the songs and helped to create the stories of the dreams. *Dreamgirls* at that time was still finding its voice—one much different from the final voice of the show the world would come to know. It was hard work creating our page in music theater history. I was just thrilled to be there and could hardly believe my luck. I pinched myself every day to make sure it was really happening.

There I was at the table with some of the most gifted women ever. And we were working together to create this story. Of course, it would be a long road to get there. I was in awe of Nell Carter. She was a big woman, with an even larger talent, who described herself as a Black, bi-sexual, Jewish singing lady. At times, a prickly personality, Nell had demons she was fighting. I was given the unofficial job of checking on Nell during rehearsals. It never crossed my mind to say, "No." I probably would have picked up everyone's laundry if they'd asked me.

Nell's behavior was at times erratic and increasingly more unpredictable. I will never forget one day when we were workshopping a song. She stood in the center of the room, belting out the lyrics in that huge, marvelous voice of hers. And then just like that, she stopped mid-note and headed out the door. Tom raised his eyebrows at me as if to say, "Follow her." So, I did.

I headed down the hall wondering where she could have gone. And then I heard the noises, strange moaning from the bathroom. I felt my heart begin to race. It sounded as if she was dying. The bathroom door was slightly ajar.

"Nell," I said. "Are you okay?"

There was more moaning. My head was spinning. *What if she was having a heart attack? What if she was dying? I would be responsible for the death of one of America's greatest talents, and the show hadn't even opened yet.* Ha! Me and my drama. With shaking hands, I pushed the door open. I felt my breath catch in my throat. There she was, that gifted, larger than life woman, filling up that tiny space, as she hunched over the toilet bowl, sobbing, and heaving. I was scared.

"Nell?" She didn't seem to know I was there. "Nell," I said again a bit louder.

Nell turned around to look at me. Her eyes were bright red, and she was covered in vomit. I will never forget the look on her face. It was more of a glare, as if she could see straight through me, as if to say: "You know absolutely nothing about the real world, little girl." Watching her, I knew she was right. She heaved herself up and came at me. "Stay away from the hard stuff," she growled and pushed me away, closing the door. I had a lot to learn.

Soon after, Nell left the workshop. She was going to Hollywood to star in a new TV sitcom, called *Gimme a Break,* where she would play the wise-cracking maid. Part of me felt relieved. That look on her face and her admonition to stay away from the hard stuff had scared me. That was the first time I had seen the reality of drug addiction, and it would not be the last. I knew that my body and voice were my instruments. They were God's gift to me. And I wasn't going to destroy them with any stuff, especially this mysterious hard stuff. And in some ways, seeing Nell like that was good for me, although her expression would continue to haunt me for decades. That was a DIVA lesson, you've heard before, but let me say it again: Don't do anything that will cause you to lose yourself, because the parts you lose today, you might need tomorrow. And more often than not, they are the most beautiful parts of you.

As soon as Nell left the show, Joseph Papp did, too. We had lost the backing of the Public Theater. Without Nell, the Tony Award winning star, his hopes of making the show into a Broadway hit would be tough and a hard-sell. He must have figured there was a much easier sale out there. Project #9 was shelved. Tom Eyen was upset. He believed in Project #9, and Tom was no quitter, so he hit the streets again, trying to find a partner who saw the same potential in this little dream project that he did.

While in limbo, I took off on another tour of duty to see the other side of the world and to sing my heart out for our troops. And this time, I was the star of the show.

Eventually, Tom found a potential partner in Michael Bennett. Michael Bennett was a superstar, fresh off of directing and choreographing the smash hit, *A Chorus Line*. Michael knew how to really work and shop a show, having done it with *A Chorus Line* to great success. Michael agreed to finance a second workshop of Project #9. Once he was on board, the project really picked up steam. The first time I met Michael, he seemed nice enough, but a bit intense. If I had only known, then what I know now.

The creation of *A Chorus Line* by Michael Bennett is stuff of Broadway legends, not to mention Broadway cautionary tales. *A Chorus Line* went on to become one of the most successful shows in Broadway history, with revival after revival for decades to come. At the heart of the musical were a series of recordings made in 1974. The participants were mostly unknown actors, dancers, and struggling hopefuls who barely made ends meet. They shared their real-life stories, allowing Michael Bennett to tape record them. These young dancers/ actors signed contracts in exchange for a single dollar. They gave away all rights to their interviews. Wayne Cilento who appeared in the original production told *The New York Times*. "We were young and stupid, we kind of signed our lives away and they exploited that. "

Most likely, many of these struggling performers held secret hopes that they would be cast in this new show by this young, hot director interviewing them. Many of their stories went word to word into the final book for *A Chorus Line*. Talented actors would portray their personal stories for decades to come, touching the hearts of rapt audiences around the world. These young actors could not know any of this at the time. They were young talented men and women, fighting for their seemingly impossible dream to make it, just like the famous refrain in the show, "God, I hope I get it. I hope I get it."

The history of these men and women and how they have been compensated for their part in creating the show has been shrouded in much mystery and legal silencing. Of these thirty-seven men and women, eight went on to star in the show when it opened on Broadway. Unfortunately, the others were left behind. *A Chorus Line* went on to earn millions. And there have been countless lawsuits for fair compensation for the real people behind the show's characters.

The majority of these thirty-seven kids were Broadway gypsies, who survived show to show. They lived packed into tiny apartments and pounded the pavements from audition to audition. They waited hopelessly and sometimes sadly for their big break. The interviews taped by Michael Bennett were of their own heartache, drama, hopes, and triumphs.

Michael Bennett was a brilliant man, able to take these raw stories and turn them into theater. Much has been written about the process of making *A Chorus Line* and the subsequent lawsuits. What is publicly known is that many of these original interviewees have been somewhat compensated, but it took decades of struggling to reach a settlement. These were kids who like so many others willingly gave up stability to pursue the uncertainty of a Broadway future. Above all, they waited for their big break, their moment to shine center stage. In so many ways, I was one of them.

Not much has been said about the creation of *Dreamgirls*, which evolved through a process that was both different and similar to that of *A Chorus Line*. Among the differences, fewer of us were involved in the creation of *Dreamgirls*. Among the similarities, we were very much a part of bringing these characters and their stories to life. And, yes, we signed the same kind of contract those *A Chorus Line* gypsies had signed. "I, Sheryl Lee Ralph, signed away my contribution to the creation of *Dreamgirls* for $1. "We were young, dumb and we were exploited. I believe to this day that we were in a way authors of the show and should have been compensated properly but who said life is fair?

The first thing Michael Bennett did was to search for a talent to fill the shoes of Nell Carter. Effie Melody White would not be an easy character to cast. Tom Eyen, always on the lookout for his Effie, went to see the musical, *Your Arms Too Short to Box with God.* Jamie Patterson, who was in the *Dreamgirls* workshop knew the lead in that musical and he became instrumental in the discovery of Jennifer Holliday and in bringing her to Tom's attention.

Jennifer was a huge talent from a small town in Texas and our experiences mirrored each other in many ways. Just as in my *Reggae* experience, she had been cast in her first Broadway show the same day she had auditioned. That had been two years earlier, and now she was 21 years old. In so many ways, we were alike. We were both talented, young Black girls with intense drive, probably both thrilled and a little scared at the sudden turn our lives had taken. Unfortunately, we would not have the opportunity to be friends until decades later.

During the evolution and first run of *Dreamgirls,* and for years after, we would be thought of as rivals.

People would hear our names and think of the word "catfight." There is some truth to every rumor but sometimes, the real truth lies much deeper. Yes, Jennifer and I were rivals, but that choice was made for us. We were never allowed to be friends because from moment one, Michael Bennett pitted us against each other because he said it made Jennifer "a better actress."

The second workshop would give us a name for the show and the gift of Jennifer Holiday who'd play Effie. Jennifer, however, left the project after some disapproval of her character and the material given for her character. She simply wanted more, and it just was not there yet. The workshop was still young, and Michael Bennett was pretty uncomfortable with the material. At the time the show was developing under the direction of Tom Eyen.

In those early days, the cast seemed to appear and disappear through a revolving door. And one day through that door came this big, bold, boisterous, and friend of mine to this day—aha—Jenifer Lewis. Yes, Jenifer Lewis joined us for a few weeks when the script was in transition. When she didn't work out, one of the stars of *Hair* was brought in, and she left just as quickly.

At that point in the show's development, Effie was an in-home nurse after she left the Dreams. Her character took care of an old Jewish lady played by Estelle Getty. The, Estelle Getty, who would go on to play Sophia in *The Golden Girls*. S. Epatha Merkerson, later of *Law and Order*, joined us as Jimmy's wife. Despite the chaos of a rotating cast, Loretta Devine and I were always around. We were there from the very beginning.

The workshops continued. By the fourth workshop, Michael Bennett had taken over as director of the show, and promptly changed the name from *Big Dreams* to *Dreamgirls*.

In the fourth workshop, we sat around the table deconstructing and reconstructing the story. We were moved from a '50s era show to a '60s era show. Michael Bennett wooed Jennifer Holliday back to the table. The rest is, as they say, theater history; or at the very least, the beginning of theater "her story."

I had a long, emotional, and turbulent relationship with Michael Bennett. Michael was a creative genius and a gift to the world of musical theater. He was a legend, and his vision will live on as each new generation discovers his masterful works. That said, he was not the easiest man in the world to deal with. And I am putting that mildly. The truth, my soon to be full-fledged DIVAs, is this: In your lifetime, you will dance with many different kinds of people, and I guarantee, some of them will step on your toes. How will you deal with these people?

Well, this took years for me to learn. And I am still learning. Without a doubt, working with Michael Bennett was a crash course in tolerance and diplomacy.

DIVA Lesson Eight
Life Isn't Always Fair, But We Play Fair Anyway.

CHAPTER NINE

BULLET PROOF

One of the main characters in *A Chorus Line* is Zach, the director, who is running an audition where he must pare down seventeen hopefuls to eight cast members. In doing so, he often berates and manipulates the actors, pushing them as far as he possibly can. He wants to see how well they handle stress. He is a perfectionist who creates by pressuring others to perform and conform to his idea of artistic perfection. He is capable of tenderness, but those moments are rare. This character is flawed, tough, and absolutely brilliant.

Just as the auditioning actors in *A Chorus Line* were based on real interviews, the director character came from real life as well, being based on Michael Bennett himself. So that notoriously tough director, who storms down the aisle in the first act and opens the show shouting, "Step, kick, kick, leap, kick, touch. Again, step, kick, kick, leap, kick, touch. Again." As the actors struggled through the difficult choreography, I knew that man—excuse me: character—well. Michael demanded a great deal of us: Our time, our talent, and our complete attention to the details of his new masterpiece.

I had learned from my first movie and the great Sidney Poitier to give the director complete attention. Yet, it seemed to me that Michael thrived in an atmosphere of self-created tension. Drama and conflict were the order of the day. Michael did everything he possibly could to put a wedge between Jennifer and me and wanted us to dislike each other. He would show blatant favoritism for me one day: Jennifer the next. He would be hot and cold to us both, often comparing us in front of the cast, and even worse, to each other.

We were both young, naive, and very aware that we had been given the greatest opportunity of our lives. And with Michael Bennett at the helm, we knew *Dreamgirls* had a good chance of becoming a huge hit. Michael could find financial backing and the talent to make the show come alive. And we knew he had the power to fire either one of us at the drop of a feather boa.

Since the Deena and Effie characters became rivals, both fighting for the limelight and at one point the same man, perhaps Michael felt that real life tension would transfer well to the stage. Or maybe he just liked the drama. Either way, the atmosphere was thick with uneasiness while the show was still evolving. Michael would regularly adjust the script. Sometimes, I would be given the juicier solos, just to have them snatched away and all attention given to Jennifer. As we grew more connected to the project and the story began to take its final shape, we became these characters. We loved, fought, and hoped for their success, as well as for the success of the show itself.

Michael could have moments of supportiveness towards us as often as we had to live with the uneasiness and fear he created. Perhaps this mythical catfight between Jennifer and me, one that we have discussed at length and even found humorous now as adult women, has somehow become prophetic for the success of the work. Urban legend says that the same catfight existed between Jennifer Hudson and Beyoncé as they were making *Dreamgirls*, the Movie, almost thirty years later.

There might have been drama backstage, but what happened on stage was much clearer. We all knew the show was something special. We could feel that magic in the air. The real question that haunted us was, "Would this show ever have an audience?"

We still didn't have full financial backing. Michael Bennett took to the streets to find someone who believed in Project #9 enough to fund the production. He partnered with David Geffen, a shrewd, handsome young man, with the most beautiful piercing blue eyes. David Geffen signed up to be one of the producers and brought in another big name: Quincy Jones. At that time, no one was bigger than Quincy Jones. He was the man behind Michael Jackson. Quincy could snap his fingers, and we would have a real, bona fide Broadway show on our hands.

Michael Bennett told us Q (that's what he called Quincy) was coming to see the complete run-through of the first act. Ha! We were so excited. This was a Black man with power—real power. Any issues Jennifer and I were having, oh, we put those aside. Quincy Jones arrived, and we excitedly waited in the rooms of 890 Broadway, with our fingers crossed.

"This is it," I whispered to sweet Loretta Devine.

"Ralph, I have a good feeling," she whispered back.

We both grinned at each other. I said a silent prayer, and I am sure she did, too.

Q was a good-looking man—alright, very handsome man. He sat in the back of the room with Michael Bennett and David Geffen, looking at the show as it played out on the huge Mylar screens before us. It was going so well. Everybody was on point. And then we went right into the scene with Jennifer's gut-wrenching rendition of "And I Am Telling You, I'm Not Going." We had rehearsed and rehearsed for this moment, all for Mr. Jones' visit.

I remember thinking how great we were all doing, and how amazed Mr. Jones must be to watch what we created. *"This is the beginning of everything,"* I thought to myself. And then it happened. As soon as we reached the point where the Dreams come back and sing, "And baby, baby, baby, you're driving me wild," and the chorus chimed in with "Show biz just a show biz," well, Quincy Jones stood up. Just like that, he stood up and walked right out of the room. Not a word of warning. Not a word of anything. Not even a thank you or goodbye. Quincy had exited the building.

All I remember is my shock as I saw the back of that expensive suit disappearing out the door. David Geffen followed right behind him. I turned to Loretta and Jennifer. I said, "But we were good." They were just as confused as I was.

"He didn't get it," Michael Bennett told me later.

"He didn't get it? But we're going to be big," I said, almost crying.

Michael just shook his head at me. Once again, I was that little girl Nell Carter had seen—the girl who knew nothing about the real world. It's just show biz, I guess.

We did not let Quincy stop us. We kept right at it. We knew that Project #9, or *Dreamgirls*, was extraordinary. It had to happen. We figured someone would eventually see the magic and want to help us.

Then we got the news that Michael had secured the funding. Our little underdog show about a trio of young Black women with big dreams, who go from being nobodies, to having everything, losing some of the important things on the way to fame—well, it was headed for the "Great White Way," or maybe, "Great Black Way" in this case. My life would never be the same.

Up to the very end Michael kept the pressure on and even on opening night he intensified his rivalry between Effie and Deena. One moment I will never forget that says it all, was on opening night. Michael Bennett gave the cast gifts. To Jennifer, Tiffany diamond earrings. For me, a bronze belt buckle, with the

Dreamgirls logo on it. A nice gift, but certainly not a
girl's best friend. I know this was a small thing, but to
this day, the small things often mean a great deal. It
hurts me now as much as it did then. For years I have
tried to understand Michael's motivation in creating
an atmosphere of tension between his real-life leading ladies.

As for Mr. Quincy Jones. I saw him again years later.
I was asked to sing as a part of a Peggy Lee tribute at the
Hollywood Bowl. My song was, "Big Spender," and I
sang my heart out in my own particular style to the
crowd of thousands underneath those stars. After the
show, Quincy came up to me and said, "You really let
it out all over that stage. You're very talented." Ha-ha! I
don't think he had any idea of that moment we shared
long ago, or that we had ever met before. For a lesser
director, Q walking out the door could have spelled
the death of the project but for Michael Bennett, a lesson I learned that I hold closely to my belt…one person
don't stop no show!

When he had first seen me in the *Dreamgirls* workshop, I had been nothing more than a young, eager
woman, desperate to impress him. I'm sure he had
encountered so many others just like me.

"Thank you," I said. And I meant it. We all make
mistakes.

In my life, I have made many choices, and I stand
by all of them. As I have said, my DIVA friends, life is
about choices—choices both big and small, all adding
up to something. One of those choices I made, a big

one, would not arrive until many years later. Despite the monetary gain from thousands of productions and a big budget movie, the cast and I didn't seek financial gain for our participation in the creation of *Dreamgirls*. Sad.

I have a great deal of respect for the choice to seek compensation by many of the original contributors to *A Chorus Line*. And I admire their strength in seeking what they were owed. I understand them more than they could ever possibly know. At some point however, the *Dreamgirls* cast decided for better or worse, that was not going to be our choice. In case you're wondering, let me set the record straight from my point of view. What it comes down to is this: Deena Jones, the character I created in *Dreamgirls*, is very much a part of me. She comes from me, Sheryl Lee Ralph. She would not exist as she is without my input.

Dreamgirls is a musical that we, meaning the actors, as much as the writers and director created. And by created, I mean, we often brought the seed of an idea to life. *Dreamgirls* began without a script. At the start there was just a cast in a room with Tom Eyen and sometimes Henry Krieger. They would give us options for songs and scenes within their concept. We took those ideas and spent hours doing improvisations that were recorded and formed into rough, scripted material and music. We would build from those rough scenes and work them into the magic they became.

This ongoing, constantly evolving process of ensemble creation was not unlike that in the creation of *A Chorus Line*. These characters emerged from the actors. So, we knew better than anyone else what these characters would or would not do. If I felt that Deena was doing something within the script that my Deena would not do, I would let it be known. Since this was a workshop, my thoughts were often taken seriously. And the material would once again be adjusted and rewritten. This would happen again and again, until we had something that resembled the *Dreamgirls* of today.

A great portion of Deena's character and dialogue, as well as the choices she makes and actions she takes throughout the script are mine. They were birthed from my own experiences as a young, Black woman, wanting nothing more than to share her talent in a big way. Like Deena, I would have struggles. And like Deena, I would survive and thrive through it all. Of course, at the time, I did not know the survive-and-thrive part of my life was to be so intensely tested in the following months. *Dreamgirls*, both the creation and the run of the show itself, would test me in ways I could never have imagined. At some point *Dreamgirls* went from belonging to any of us to becoming theater that belonged to the world and even now inspires the world of the arts.

"We are your dream girls. Boys, we'll make you happy." Years later, watching the lines I had written come out of the mouth of Beyoncé on the big screen— well, that was a moment I found both strange and surreal. No matter what, one thing will never change.

I will forever be grateful for what *Dreamgirls* taught me and the impact the musical has had on the world and on me. Being part of creating that show, for the *Dreamgirls* universe, is something I hold dear.

For me, money will not change anything. I just know this. I would not trade those experiences, the best and the worst moments of my life; the ecstasy or the disappointments I've done for anything in the world. One last thing: all the years since, one thought has always been with me; one day I will share my *Dreamgirls* experiences with the world, with hopes they will offer insight and inspiration to those who read them and continue to dream big. And no amount of money in the world is more important than that. And this is one of the reasons I wrote this book.

▼

DIVA Lesson Nine
Never, Ever, Ever Give Up On Your Dreams!

CHAPTER TEN

RAIN ON MY PARADE

ooking back, starring in *Dreamgirls* on Broadway gave me some of the best times in my life. It also gave me the most horrific times. No one is born a DIVA, my friends. A real DIVA becomes DIVA through experience. A real DIVA, that Divinely Inspired Victoriously Alive person whose roots come from the Latin word for goddess, is not born a DIVA. She or he is born with the potential for DIVA-hood. And getting there is not always easy. Real DIVAs, like everybody else, have their highs and lows. Real DIVAs make mistakes and learn from them. Real DIVAs, the kind we are, my friends can stumble gracefully on the road of life.

I was barely in my twenties, and I was starring on Broadway. In the next few years, I would have moments of triumph unlike anything I could have imagined. I would have those stumbles, too. Some of those stumbling moments would turn into outright trips and staggering falls. The best DIVA training of all was learning to get up, dust myself off, and keep moving forward on the road of life.

"When Broadway history is being made, you can feel it," read *The New York Times* on December 21, 1981. My life changed overnight. We were a smash...a success...a bonafide hit! It was the most exciting time I could remember. In some ways, the experience is a blur of images and emotions. There we were on that grand stage of the Imperial Theatre. The audiences were right there with us. Night after night, they rose to their feet showering us with thunderous applause—the kind of applause that lets you know that you are loved—really, truly loved.

This revolutionary musical starring Black women was a hit the likes of which Broadway had not seen in years. We went from praying for backers and believers to having sold-out houses with a year of advanced ticket sales. Our pictures were splashed on magazine covers and newsstands across New York, London, and even Tokyo. There were television appearances and rave reviews. Our show had touched people with freshness and originality.

Dreamgirls spoke to anyone who had ever had a dream; anyone who ever had big hopes and even bigger obstacles. This was a show about making your way and succeeding, even if the world told you, it was impossible. That was a message that seemed to reach people. Fans ranged from children seeing their first musical; to young women finding their own dreams;

to gay men who secretly wanted to be a member of the Dreams; to the stay-at-home matinee mom and the A-list movie star. Everybody found something to love in *Dreamgirls*.

Dreamgirls exploded. We were the toast of the town—the belles of the ball on Broadway. We had our celebrity fans, like Michael Jackson, who came to see the show again, and again, and again. Luther Vandross who was in the audience more times than I can remember went from being a fan to a friend. And he remained a friend until the time of his passing.

I would be in the show for 1,247 performances, but I would have a lifetime of experiences. This would be one of the most magical and confusing times of my life. This was also the beginning of a crazy time in New York. A time when stars can lose their way.

It was the height of Studio 54 days, and I was invited everywhere. Lavish engagements and gorgeous dinner affairs took place after the show. I was welcomed with open arms by people. Sometimes by White people who would never have given a Black woman the time of day before they saw *Dreamgirls*. Legendary parties were held at Michael Bennett's Central Park South apartment. Everyone wanted to be there: celebrities, politicians, famous actors, and musicians. You felt lucky to get an invitation. Whatever Michael was feeling about me at the time, I was often invited. *Dreamgirls* was his prize show after all, and he called me one of his stars. If anything, he liked to show off his stars as a physical manifestation of his success.

I will never forget those parties. You never knew what to expect. Would it be a straight crowd or a gay crowd? Businessmen and their mistresses? Hollywood A-Listers? Rich men with their beautiful young trophy boys? Cougars and their hot, young cubs? The whole experience was overwhelming and eye-opening. And then there was the sudden reality that this was a world I had never really seen before. There was sex and drugs at the purest levels and believe me, the world of sex and drugs can be a dangerous mixture. Throw in a little alcohol for an extra kick on the elevator ride down. In my wildest imagination, I could never have pictured the amount of cocaine I saw at parties all across Manhattan, all for the taking or sniffing. It would often be elegantly presented, piled high like miniature snow mountains on silver trays. Beautiful people would cut it with the precision of artists, and arrange lines so fast, their hands were a blur.

Drugs were never my thing. Thank God! And if I even thought of losing my marbles, I could still hear Nell Carter saying, "Stay away from the hard stuff." If I were ever tempted—and it was easy to be tempted—I'd just recall Nell Carter's face in that bathroom covered in vomit, red, vacant eyes staring at me. I'd just remember how crack cocaine literally took the beauty and life away from one of my childhood friends. I'd remember how unattractive drunk and high girls looked. But most of all I'd remember what my mother told me for years: "Don't leave your drink anywhere, ever. And if you smoke you will ruin your voice and smell bad. And never, ever, ever put anything up your nose." Case closed.

I am not sure how I stayed strong with all of those people pushing drugs on me and at me. But somehow, I did. No is a full sentence, always. And this crowd, full of people who influenced audiences for a living—well, they could be persistent. But I kept thinking, I have a show to do and that was as much high as I needed. Being strong in the face of this type of temptation would be hard for anyone and it would only be the first of many tests. But, knowing who you are inside and out, your values and the lines never to cross go a long way in a world of beautifully orchestrated chaos.

I understand young Hollywood stars and the temptations they face because I faced them all. I was young and suddenly thrust into the limelight. Lord knows I made some stupid choices. And not surprisingly, some of those stupid choices involved men.

I had plenty of admirers. All sorts of men came out of the woodwork to date a real, live Dream Girl. Some pursued me intensely, but I was picky. Not to mention that I hardly had time to sleep performing eight grueling shows a week. Plus, I was doing double duty on the CBS soap opera *Search for Tomorrow* during the day and *Dreamgirls* at night. This DIVA was booked, busy and exhausted. So, dating and parties were not my priorities. Nonetheless, I was just as susceptible to a handsome face as any woman in her early twenties.

God knows I had my pick. Starring in a hit Broadway show meant I was never at a lack for suitors and admirers. But were they interested in me, Sheryl Lee Ralph, or the beautiful dream, Deena Jones? That was the question. Yes, a great deal of myself was in the character of Deena and as her popularity soared through the course of the musical, my own real-life journey began mirroring her experiences. In reality however, Deena and I were very different. See, Deena had decades of experience, lived, and learned in every two and half hour show on the stage. On the other hand, when I stepped out that stage door every night, I was still in my early twenties, and in some ways, more innocent than my years.

Of course, I didn't say no to every stage door Johnny. I dated quite a few handsome men. There was the famous musician, who would get recognized wherever we went. He was kind of kinky, and I just couldn't keep up with all of that. The television actor who was almost too attractive for his own good, sometimes getting distracted by his own reflection in shop windows when we walked down the street. I had to laugh at it because it was fun and funny. I never took any of those guys too seriously and I'm glad I didn't because these were the '80s, when playing musical beds was as acceptable as playing Monopoly. But all of that would suddenly change when sex became synonymous with death.

The AIDS epidemic hit Broadway like a bomb blast—the tremors of which we are still feeling to this day. In a short time, everything would change forever. Looking back now, I am glad I took my time, because sleeping or hooking up with someone too quickly is the fastest way to mess up what could be a meaningful relationship. For my younger DIVAs, remember A DIVA knows their worth, and *they* are worth waiting for. If the person really matters to you, take your time, and give it time. On some level, I knew that even then. But as the old saying goes, "When love is the last thing you are looking for, it might just tap you on your shoulder and say, 'Here I am.'"

Here I am, arrived, and the tap was loud. He was an advertising executive who'd seen me perform. He sent me flowers and a gift, and I said yes to a date with a man more than twenty years my senior. Now, here's the thing about dating pretty young things, especially those in the public's eye; they don't always know who they are themselves as yet and can be influenced. Surrounded by publicists, agents, fans, and yes, men and women—an entourage of yes people who make a living off of their success, they are buried under an avalanche of false praise and adoration. Many of them start in show business early, and never have the opportunity to live regular young lives before they become a "name" or the next hot thing. That combination of success, insecurity, and a staff telling you that you are the greatest thing since sliced bread, can be a recipe for disaster. We've seen it happen over and over with the same results.

So, back to the love story. Here is this sophisticated older man courting me. The first thing that struck me was that unlike some of the younger men I dated, he knew himself through and through. He knew he was a man and was confident in his accomplishments. He was a successful man who'd worked hard for his success. Well-traveled, he had seen the world and had real-life experiences my young mind couldn't begin to fathom. He was dashing and well-spoken. He wasn't a boy. We could have an actual conversation and he was interested in my views on the world and had things he could teach me. Oh, yes! And the part I haven't mentioned is that he treated me like an absolute princess. In his eyes, I was a treasure to be handled carefully, adored, and fully appreciated at every moment—even if I was only ten years older than his daughter.

And, yes, he was handsome—not in the pretty boy way I was used to with the man boys I had been seeing, but in a way that could not be missed. When this man entered a room he owned it, and he had picked me.

To top it all off, this man had money—real money. And he wasn't afraid to spoil me. These were the kinds of dates you only read about in romance novels: a limo waiting for me after a show, to whisk me off to a private table in the most luxurious, exclusive restaurants in the city—the kind that had a six-month waiting list to get in. Sudden surprise trips on my rare days off to a private island, where his chef would cook us delicious meals, and we would walk on our own beach at sunset. Huh! You can't make this stuff up.

I was completely, utterly taken with the whole experience. I thought I was head over Manolo Blahniks in love. Of course, my brain might have been a little clouded and my glasses a little rosy. That was the beginning of a truly important DIVA lesson. A DIVA deserves to feel good in all aspects of life, from the bedroom to the boardroom and every place in between. And a real man or woman, one worthy of a DIVA, is not afraid to make sure they feel real good. DIVAs, if you work hard on yourself to achieve a DIVA-worthy level of confidence and stature, well, you will know you are worth that adoration, so pick people who are suitable and appreciative of you. They will know they are blessed to be with you. And so will you. You should be loved. Don't be tolerated, be celebrated. You deserve it.

So maybe it was infatuation, but I truly believed I had found my Prince Charming. We were seeing each other for quite a while, and everyone could see me changing—even on stage. I would feel this man's presence and channel all of that emotion into Deena. When Deena sang her love, well, that was Sheryl Lee Ralph singing her own. I was so happy, but relatively inexperienced in the reality of relationships. While my college friends had been looking to get married, I had been looking towards my career and getting my stardom on. While other actors in L.A. had been living the swinging '80s lifestyle, I had still been looking towards my career. And now I was in my early twenties, and this was my first, serious love affair. Needless to say, I didn't yet know how to read all of the signals. When I got too close, he would back away. The scenario repeated itself. We would get closer and then he would stop returning my calls. But I was seeing the world through a filter of young love, and I would keep calling.

You've been there. Admit it!

I would continue to let him make plans and cancel them on me. It was the classic bad-boyfriend scenario, and I had to break that cycle. It took me truly valuing myself to know when to walk away. Now that sounds good, but the truth is, in the end, he actually pushed me away from him. He knew I was the marrying kind. And at this point, I fully owned that I lived to be a mother one day. That was not at all what he wanted. He had his children and was set in not wanting any more. And he had taken steps to make sure it did not happen. Snip. A family with an adoring younger girlfriend was not at all what he wanted.

During another fantasy date, he set the scene for the breakup.

"You deserve to have the joy of motherhood and you won't get that with me."

He was right. Still, I was willing to give up that dream, just to be with him. Dumb.

"So, this is where it ends," he said, dropping the keys to our beautiful suite on the table. The keys dropped and so did my heart. "Enjoy the weekend. Everything's paid for." He walked out without a good-bye kiss, hug, or anything.

I was devastated and depressed. I had just been dumped. Even though he dumped me in the lap of luxury, it didn't hurt any less. Painful experiences will mold you into a stronger woman. Of course, when you're eating a pint or two of Häagen-Dazs with tears rolling down your face, it feels as if the world is coming to an end. But it won't, my DIVA friends. I promise you, it won't. When I look at the two beautiful children I have today, I only thank God, he dumped me. I didn't see back then that the choice he made for me was indeed love. But one has to know who they are to be able to walk away from anything and as I said, he knew himself through and through.

Cry it out. Scream, pray, wish for a miracle, then get out of bed and start all over again. Dress yourself up in your dreams. Put on your lipstick and throw away your fears. Something even better is right around the corner. Do not dwell on it too long. Let it be lipstick and lashes under the bridge, DIVA.

I have always dated for love, not money or material goods. I have seen all of those women who dated men thinking they were going to get something. Some became the Baby-Mama, thinking it would make him stay and also put money in their bank account. Some just wanted to see and be seen. All of that just wasn't my style. Sometimes actresses date to further their careers. Now, that might open the door, but you had better have the guts and talent to stay in the room, not to mention you have to be careful. The industry is not always pretty and not always kind. And there is always the risk that you could end up folded in a suitcase and put out with the trash. Oh, yes, it has happened. Screwed and put out like garbage.

For better or worse, better I truly believe, I was looking for my love story. Unfortunately, most times the love story doesn't end the way it does in fairytales. Often you are left without the glass slipper, crying yourself to sleep, and wondering why you keep falling for the Princess's bad seed brother with commitment issues. But in the end, you learn. And in the end, you love and get loved in return.

I wouldn't' fully come to understand the signs or see that I'd been picking the wrong men until years later. But I would eventually realize, and that would make all the difference in my finding lasting happiness. In observation mode I would be able to discern charm without intelligence, even if he were fine. Gifts given to get something without the appreciation of the real me. Guys who could talk a good game but would duck and run at crunch time. Now I know how to recognize those signs that a guy is just wrong.

I found my lasting love. I look at my husband now, and I see a smart man with genuine kindness, a big heart, and a love for me that is true and pure. A love that comes from an appreciation for who I am at my core. I look at him and know he will take me for better or worse and love me through the good and the bad. I look at that man, and I see a great politician, who lives to make the world a better place, a man who knows I am an important part of his well-being, his happiness, and his success. Love can be complicated but true love prevails, and I wouldn't have me any other way. I look at my man and know I am loved, and that I deserve it. His love gives me wings.

That, my DIVAs, is what makes all of the difference!

▼

**DIVA Lesson Ten
Love Gives You Wings to Soar, Not Pain.**

CHAPTER ELEVEN

CIRCLE OF FRIENDS

As I look back, my days in *Dreamgirls* were some of the greatest and most challenging times of my life. For the good times, I am eternally grateful for having had the opportunity to reach audiences every night, to see their faces light up with joy as they watched us on stage, to move them to tears, to touch them, to lift them up, and to give them hope was a gift. Being part of such an iconic show was a blessing. *Dreamgirls* was revolutionary.

Finally, there was a stage full of beautiful Black women. They were no stereotypes nor background characters. They, the beautiful Black people, were the show itself. To be a part of creating something so ahead of its time and something that would open the door for countless young Black actresses and actors everywhere for years to come is something I am proud to have been a part of. Opening doors that have never been open, well, it is not always pretty or welcoming on the other side.

Those early *Dreamgirls* days would offer a lifetime of lessons. And some of those lessons would be painful. More wake-up calls would occur in that short of a span than most women have in their entire twenties. I have always been overly trusting of people. I had been raised in a community who looked out for me and believed in heartfelt kindness. Even in difficult experiences in Hollywood, I have kept faith that people were genuinely good at heart. They struggled as we all do. I believed that if they said they wanted the best for you, well, they meant it. That, my DIVA friends, is an unfortunate lesson to learn because it is not always true. Like with love, you have to find the good people—the ones who really want the best for you—and hold them close. Getting fooled, well, that's just part of the learning process on how to find them. *Dreamgirls* taught me some early lessons about sisterhood, and they were not always easy to learn. But my mother taught the importance of sisterhood and in sisterhood I believe.

I am a proud member of Delta Sigma Theta Sorority. Watching my sorority sisters go out into the world and triumph is extremely satisfying. Their successes are my successes. There is power in belonging to a community of women whose works and beliefs you respect. Having women with whom to speak your mind is vital in staying emotionally sane. And any DIVA knows, if mama don't feel good, nobody feels good.

Backstabbing, demeaning, and trying to undermine the success of your sisters, well, it seems plain crazy to me. That is why I celebrate all women who celebrate sisterhood—no matter what colors they are, no matter what colors they wear: Crimson and cream, pink and green, blue, and white, blue, and gold, and any combination thereof. I celebrate sisterhood.

Black women have always had to work harder than anyone else. We left the African continent under pain and duress and were put to backbreaking work throughout the American continent, in fact world-wide. This is what we did, do, and are—working women. We did our share, more than our share, and then kept going, because we did not have a choice. When our great-great-grandmothers were out there working in those fields and they just happened to be pregnant, well, they did not have a choice. They could not take time off to recharge. There was no mater-nity leave. They dropped those babies in the hot sun, wrapped them up, strapped them to their backs, and resumed work. They did not have time for petty wor-ries or nasty behavior. They had better things to do, like survive. Those are the women we come from. This is our legacy, and I have been taught not to forget it. You shouldn't forget it either. Someone picked cotton for my dream to come true. And they did it together. Anything else is brainwashing...you can reject it. Sis-terhood is the way to rise. Women who support and respect other women are to be praised.

So here I was on a grander stage, literally, than I could ever have imagined. There were so few roles for Black women out there and I'd landed one of the best. Unfortunately, not every woman in the entertainment industry was thrilled for me. Like they say, haters are going to hate. But I truly believe that when women work together and support each other, there is a lot of power in that. And that kind of power can change the world for the better.

Diana Ross was not happy with the show. Now, this made me sad, because I loved and admired her for as long as I could remember. But now, she was angry at what she believed was my portrayal of her. She wasn't afraid to tell everyone, including the major publications, that she felt our show was a blatant rip-off of her own rise to stardom. *Dreamgirls* was her story," she said.

No matter how many times I said that I was not playing Diana Ross, the urban legend ruled, Drreamgirls was the story of the Supremes. I worshipped Ms. Ross, but I knew that our story was completely original. Project #9 was based on the pure creativity of actors around a table in those early workshops. The cast experiences, our own highs and lows were the emotional center of the script, not to mention there was the perfect plot for every great musical or movie: boy meets girl, boy loses girl, and boy gets her back again—a journey that speaks to us all.

Now, I'd heard the things she said about the story, and I heard what she said about me. But let me be clear here: I love, adore, and admire Ms. Diana Ross—then and now. Okay. I had even once snuck into her dressing room, like little Eve Harrington, one summer at the Westbury Music Fair. Not to mention, my father always said I should only believe half of what you see and none of what you hear, because sometimes gossip and hearsay is just that. Shade.

As for the rise to stardom being Diana's story, well, of course, she could relate to it. It was the story of so many Black, gifted girls with big talent and even bigger dreams. It was the story that created Motown and The Sound of Philadelphia and California Soul. Yes, the Supremes were in there, but so were The Shirelles, The Three Degrees, the Ronettes, LaBelle, the Shirelles and many, many other Black gifted female singers who fought to get the recognition they deserve. This story was our legacy as Black performers and the legacy of brave pioneers who brought R&B and soul music right out of the background and to the world. Mary Wilson of the Supremes understood that and embraced the show as something to be proud of. Although she admitted that some moments felt familiar, she was very public in her belief that *Dreamgirls* is a work of art and an excellent one at that. She remained proud of *Dreamgirls* until her passing. She'd often tell me, "Sheryl Lee Ralph, I'm the original Dream Girl," with a big smile spread across her face.

"No," I would say. "You're the original Supreme. I am the original Dream Girl." I loved Mary. And either way, we are both proud of having been a part of something iconic: Her, with the Supremes and me with *Dreamgirls*. The truth is any woman with a dream she is hell bent on realizing is a Dream Girl!

Women have extraordinary power when they have each other's back. They lose more when they choose to knife each other in the back. Being upset because another woman has success says more about you than anything else. You might have heard someone utter the phrase, "Humph, she thinks she's all that." Well, what that person is really saying is, "I am none of all that." Now here is an important DIVA lesson for you. A DIVA does not enter a room saying, "Look at me. Look at me." A real DIVA knows that she is someone to be looked at and finds the grace to own the room.

Diana Ross is Diana Ross, and everyone turns to look when Diana Ross enters the room. So, when she entered the Russian Tea Room, I was there having lunch with my agent. I was thrilled! Besides just seeing this gorgeous woman with that huge halo of hair within a few feet of me, I think my brain momentarily stopped working. All I could think was, *That's Diana Ross. That's Diana Ross. That is really her.*

I stood up and walked right over to her. "Ms. Ross," I said.

She stopped and turned around dramatically with that gleaming smile of hers. There she was the great Ms. Diana Ross for whom I would stay up late to watch on the *Ed Sullivan Show*—right there in front of me. And she was stunning. She seemed to glow. I had to speak to her.

"I'm Sheryl Lee Ralph."

She cut me off instantly. The smile disappeared from her face. It just seemed to melt clear away. The whole room seemed to go quiet, like in the movies. Or at least it seemed that way to me.

"I know who you are," she said, glaring at me. "You're from that show."

The way she said "that show" was jarring and the look she gave me put a chill on everybody's vodka. The room was truly quiet. With that, she turned and walked away from me. Yes, *Dreamgirls* would open my eyes to the real world and sometimes you had to look at it through tears. That day I was sad and struggled to understand the cold shoulder I was given. Even if it were her story, which it truly wasn't, shouldn't she be happy for its success? Happy for the Black women who raised the ceiling of opportunity on Broadway?

I saw Ms. Diana Ross again in Jamaica where she was performing at the Air Jamaica's Jazz and Blues Festival. She was with three of her beautiful children. Her youngest son, Evan, is not only talented but seemed to have the heart of an angel. He didn't like the stories he had heard so he went out of his way to make sure his mother and I reintroduced ourselves and talked woman to woman. After a few awkward seconds, Diana and I found something we both cared about deeply: Our children.

During that conversation, we went from being "rivals" to something far more important than any show or song. We were simply two mothers. We had a pleasant chat about what really matters and how our children are the loves of our lives. We talked about our pride in nurturing our young to be strong, loving, good adult men and women. I can give Diana Ross a compliment, and it is the highest compliment I could ever give anyone. She has raised some wonderful children. And that is not easy whether in the spotlight or not.

I don't remember the details of petty, backstage *Dreamgirls* fights. But what I do remember and what will forever be ingrained in my consciousness are the moments that really matter. I had been so excited to get the call that I had been nominated for the prestigious Antoinette Perry Award, aka the Tony. I immediately called my parents. My mind went into overdrive wondering, *What would I wear to the nomination luncheon? And who would I take as my date?* Then the moment I found out that we had all been nominated except for Loretta Devine, a woman with her own brand of divine magic, I instantly went from Cloud Mine to heartbroken. I wanted to take this walk with her. We had been on this journey together since the very beginning. And my exhilaration was suddenly cut with a sharp sadness. This was a sisterhood, and the power of sisterhood would prevail.

Like us, Michael Bennett had been so distressed that he threw his own awards party for Loretta, which of course we all attended. And that was a most wonderful and gratifying occasion. Being able to celebrate all of the hard work that had led to the success of *Dreamgirls* and doing so with all the *Dreamgirls* sisters was a true award. I wouldn't have had it any other way.

Do I remember the specifics of the childish arguments between Jennifer Holliday and me? No. Because they were just that: childish. We were not really that far out of our girlhood ourselves. But what still makes me glow with pride and will be with me forever, is sitting next to her at the premiere of one of the reincarnations of *Dreamgirls* that hit the road. The lights went down in the theater. The show began, and Jennifer took my hand. She whispered. Her voice full of sincerity, "Sheryl, if we only knew then what we know now."

"Yes, and I am telling you. If only."

Those are the moments that matter. The ones of friendship and love and bonds that can never be severed. Those are the ones I keep close. As I said, DIVAs don't hang on to anger. Let it go and be lipstick and eyelashes under the bridge.

Fame can be a double-edged sword. Our growing success seemed to make Michael Bennett uneasy. The more popular we became, the more neurotic he became. Unfortunately, because of his death in 1987 from the dreaded disease, AIDS that decimated the Arts and Broadway, I would never get the same closure with Michael as I did with Diana Ross when I saw her in Jamaica. The more packed houses and rave reviews, the more manipulative Michael turned with the cast. Even moments such as the one with Diana, the devastation of having her speak out against us was publicity. And publicity brought in audiences. And the more audiences and acclaim, the higher the box office sales, and the more insecure and unstable Michael became. He seemed to me to have unraveled. Few would talk about or do anything about what was happening to the genius behind our hit show, especially since he signed directly or indirectly the paychecks.

No matter how popular we got, Michael had a way of making me feel with one throwaway comment or perfectly timed sneer, that I just was not good enough. He was the star. Never mind we were singing and sweating to packed houses every night, he still took some sort of twisted pleasure in hurting us. For some reason, I was his favorite target. Maybe because strong-willed as I am, I would often stand up for myself and others. I refused to cower under that man's dictatorship. That made him even more furious with me at times, and it would only get worse. But *Dreamgirls* was just rehearsal for what climbing the proverbial ladder of success and retaining one sense of identity and dignity means. You have to face it all; the good, the miraculous, the bad and the downright ugly. Michael Bennett in the end had taught me that pressure makes diamonds.

▼

DIVA Lesson Eleven
There Is Power In Sisterhood and That Kind of
Power Can Change the World for The Better.

CHAPTER TWELVE

AND THE BEAT GOES ON

Since my film debut in the movie *A Piece of the Action*, I have had a stellar career where according to IMBD I have been in 23 films, 48 television productions, 3 Broadway musicals including *Wicked,* where I made theater history as the first Black woman to play the role of Madame Morrible on Broadway. I've sung on five albums and voiced several video games and cartoons. I have produced two Broadway productions, directed, and written for the stage, had a radio show, a podcast and dear to my heart is *Divas Simply Singing,* the longest consecutive running musical AIDS Health benefit in the country, now in its 32nd year. I have won many awards and recognition throughout my career, all for which I am grateful. I know only too well that fame can sometimes be a recipe for disaster.

For sure fame can be intoxicating. Through the years I have watched so many lose their way on the way to fame, and it is always heartbreaking. I feel it safe to say that when you anchor your values and do all you can to love, respect and empower yourself, getting to know yourself from the inside out lessens the risk and the payback is invaluable.

September 12, 2022, my life and career were elevated to new heights as I stepped onto the stage of the Microsoft Theater in Los Angeles California as only the second black woman in television history to receive the Emmy for Outstanding Supporting Actress in a Comedy Series, playing the role of Mrs. Barbara Howard in the ABC smash hit *Abbott Elementary*. *Abbott Elementary* was created by Quinta Brunson, a 32 year old creative force to be reckoned with—a young black woman who made everything I went through—every door I kicked in, every wall I climbed over, every glass ceiling I attempted to break, worth it. *Abbott Elementary* was written for us, by us and ended up being loved by the world. In this role I was perfect just as I am and forever grateful.

Just like in *Dreamgirls* I stood center stage under the bright lights to thunderous applause experiencing a surreal moment; suspended in time. It was a crowning moment where I had once again been recognized for my work and I cried. Yes, I did because it has been a long, long road and it was love and faith that had brought me to this moment in time. As the audience rose to their feet, cheering me on, the love I felt was like an avalanche of joy. Even with the red lights flashing, signaling my time was up, STOP NOW, STOP NOW, I had a DIVA moment. I had earned the right to take up space and I did. I belonged there and I don't know where it all came from, but I would later read that, "Sheryl Lee Ralph just gave the most moving acceptance speech in Emmy history."

I looked out at the audience giving me a standing ovation and I knew at that moment I had to share my artists truth. Falling back on my roots I stood center stage and burst into song. A song that had always spoken truth to power for me, "Endangered Species" written by my friend the breathtaking virtuoso, Dianne Reeves.

I am an endangered species, but I sing no victim song. I am a woman. I am an artist and I know where my voice belongs.

Knowing where my voice belongs, I wanted every young and young at heart person watching to know that their dreams were worth the struggle to make it just as mine were.

"To anyone who has ever, ever had a dream and thought your dream wasn't, shouldn't, wouldn't, couldn't come true, I am here to tell you that this is what believing looks like this. This is what striving looks like."

The outpouring of love I received in the days, weeks and months following my Emmy win kept me in tears and in awe. My house was a floral jungle. It took four men and a truck to deliver the flowers sent to me from the one and only Oprah, and I wish you could have seen the delicate floral arrangement sent to me from Beyoncé with a beautifully written note that said, "To the original Dreamgirl." Not to mention the flowers and limited-edition Dom Perignon from Cynthia Erivo and Lena Waithe. Prolific rapper Kid Cudi sent me flowers so beautiful and ethereal they seem like they could levitate. Yvonne Orji sent me an arrangement where the flowers submerged in and out of the water were all blooming beautifully like something unreal. Flowers that looked heavenly. Stunning arrangements from so many beautiful people. Channing Dungey, Chairman of Warner Brothers, sent a floral arrangement from a fairytale and a vintage bottle of Dom Perignon; Pearlena Igbokwe, Chairman of Universal Studio Group, sent me not only a beautiful arrangement but a note that reminded me she had greenlit my very first script. My sorority, sister friend, and Oscar nominee, Aunjenue Ellis, gifted me the most beautiful turquoise and diamond earrings saying, "Soror, these will never fade." And neither will our friendship. Months after the Emmy Award Ceremony I was still receiving messages, phone calls, and flowers and listening to messages I had missed. Thank you. Thank you. Thank you all.

Thank you to Jamaica, the island of my mother's birth for conferring me with the Order of Jamaica and for changing my name to The Honorable Sheryl Lee Ralph. My mother in heaven is so proud to see me with this honor since she herself was The Honorable Ivy Ralph, Order of Distinction.

Indeed, it has been a long journey but here I am once again fully appreciating that I have made the right choices for my life and my career. Through it all, the good, the sometimes bad and the ugly, I stayed the course, I ran the race, and I did not ever give up. I thought about it a few times...giving up that is, but I never did. And don't you ever, ever give up on you either! And all these years later, this DIVA, Divinely Inspired, Victoriously Anointed woman has reached a point in her career where she could finally say, "I have done some good things with this talent and life I was given." But know that without you all cheering me on I could not have done it alone. I thank you.

The mentors and support I have received over my career have landed in a place where with my success and recognition, I am able to help young actors, young entrepreneurs, and the young at heart people who themselves are now breaking new barriers. I have been a warrior in the hard-fought struggle for change, change for women, change for Black people, especially black women, and other people of color waiting in the wings for their moment to shine. And not just in show business but on the world stage sharing their talents and superpower with us.

When a young actor comes up to me now and asks, "How did you do it? You have been such an inspiration." I say, "I didn't lie down, I didn't give up, I didn't roll over. I just kept it moving." Times have changed and the digital era has made accessibility one click away and fame is now happening at lightning speed.

And so, you my dear DIVA in training—DIVA as in Divinely Inspired, Victoriously Alive, seize every moment given to you. Stay the course, stay in love, stay true to yourself, do the work, and most of all, be as kind as you can for as long as you can...to as many people as you can because the same butt you kick today, you may have to kiss tomorrow. Wise words. Give back to all who seek and take the time to pay it forward. And when in doubt, give God the wheel.

But my lovelies, as you can imagine, my phone is ringing so, if you'll excuse me now, I have a lot more work to do.

▼

DIVA Lesson Twelve
The First Step Towards Being Great
Is Being Grateful!

And Remember DIVAS:

1. God can do in 60 sec. what you can't do in a lifetime…give God the wheel!
2. You matter more than you can imagine, you are enough.
3. Sometimes you just have to do *it* yourself. Every time you wait on someone else to do it for you, you give up your power. Own your power.
4. Life is very short; shower the people you love with love, especially yourself.
5. Big or small, you have influence, use it wisely.
6. Everybody does not need the mic.
7. Talk to and take time to encourage young people.
8. When you think your peace of mind is out of reach, you are not alone, get a checkup from neck up.
9. The past is in the past, the future has not arrived, but the present is right here, right now and what a gift it is.
10. When you know that you have been blessed, it is up to you to bless those around you. Just be a blessing.
11. Sometimes it's the thing you fear doing most that once you do it, it might actually make you stronger, but be careful.
12. The world will keep spinning when you stop.